Into the Jungle!

Cultures of Childhood

Susan Honeyman, Series Editor

University Press of Mississippi / Jackson

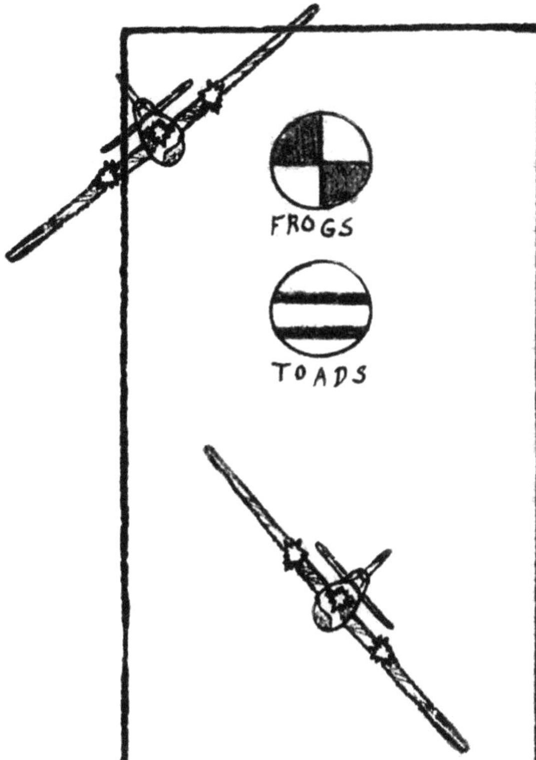

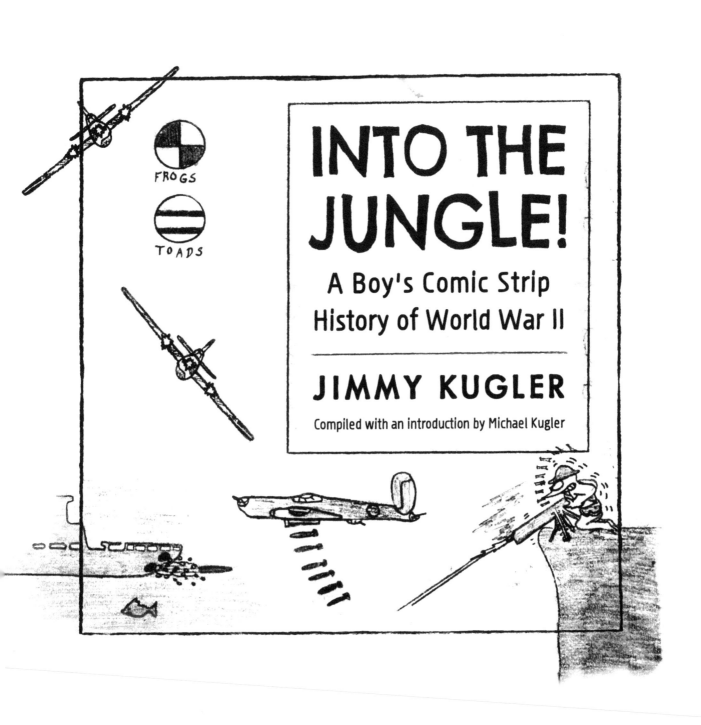

INTO THE JUNGLE!

A Boy's Comic Strip History of World War II

JIMMY KUGLER

Compiled with an introduction by Michael Kugler

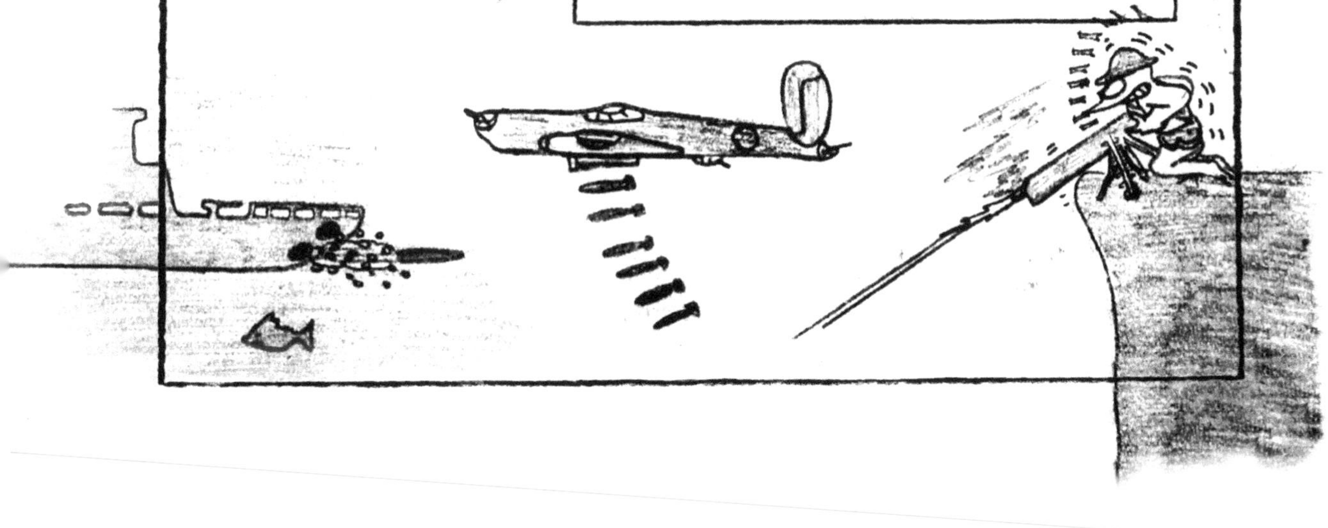

The University Press of Mississippi is the scholarly publishing agency of the Mississippi Institutions of Higher Learning: Alcorn State University, Delta State University, Jackson State University, Mississippi State University, Mississippi University for Women, Mississippi Valley State University, University of Mississippi, and University of Southern Mississippi.

www.upress.state.ms.us

The University Press of Mississippi is a member of the Association of University Presses.

First printing 2023
∞

Library of Congress Cataloging-in-Publication Data

Names: Kugler, Jimmy, 1932–1969, author. | Kugler, Michael (Michael James), writer of introduction.
Title: Into the jungle! : a boy's comic strip history of World War II / Jimmy Kugler, Michael Kugler.
Other titles: Cultures of childhood.
Description: Jackson : University Press of Mississippi, 2023. | Series: Cultures of childhood | Includes bibliographical references and index.
Identifiers: LCCN 2022051840 (print) | LCCN 2022051841 (ebook) | ISBN 9781496842817 (hardback) | ISBN 9781496842824 (trade paperback) | ISBN 9781496842831 (epub) | ISBN 9781496842848 (epub) | ISBN 9781496842855 (pdf) | ISBN 9781496842862 (pdf)
Subjects: LCSH: World War, 1939–1945—Caricatures and cartoons. | Cartoonists—Nebraska.
Classification: LCC D745.2 .K845 2023 (print) | LCC D745.2 (ebook) | DDC 940.5302/07—dc23/eng/20221207
LC record available at https://lccn.loc.gov/2022051840
LC ebook record available at https://lccn.loc.gov/2022051841

British Library Cataloging-in-Publication Data available

For Dad (1932–1969) and Mom (1935–2017);
for Cheryl, Steve, Tamara, Sarah, and James: you know the stories

Contents

Acknowledgments

Early in my thinking about this project, friends like Dan Beaver, Lendol Calder, and Mike Gambone encouraged my odd vision for making some sense of my father's adolescent comic strips. This project began over a decade ago with the research supported first by a Northwestern College Summer Research Grant. The college also supported my travel to deliver papers on it. Staff at the Dawson County Historical Museum were very helpful, and recently, Crystal Wegner was more than generous with her time and permission to reproduce images from their collection. The staff in Special Collections at Michigan State University expertly offered advice to guide my research.

The completed project was not possible without the remarkable and kind staff overseeing Northwestern's interlibrary loan system. Ben Karnish and, later, Sara Huyser tracked down request after request of odd books on comics, popular culture, and propaganda and film during World War Two.

The first published essay of this research appeared in *The Northwestern Review* thanks to the support and editorial help of Doug Anderson and Greta Grond. James Marten, editor of the *Journal of the History of Childhood and Youth*, saw through publication a brief version of this research. From the start, his editorial advice and cheer gave me confidence that this was more than just a son paying homage to his long-gone father.

After using this article in a college course, Susan Honeyman contacted me. She asked if I was thinking of publishing the comics and later brought me into contact with the UPM people. Her encouragement and enthusiasm never flagged, and I'm grateful to her. She also introduced me to Paul Karasik, whose own work on unusual or "outsider" comic books gave me models for this project. Paul's further interest and encouragement, and his own work on my dad's comics, reaffirmed the worth of this book. Working alongside Valerie Jones, Mary Heath, and all the editorial and marketing associates at UPM has been a complete joy. Debbie Burke, the editor tasked with wrangling my prose into something readable and tracking down citations, did so diligently, and with patience and good humor. Thank you, Debbie.

My colleagues here at Northwestern—Duane Jundt, Randy Jensen, Rebecca Koerselman, Sam Martin, Don Wacome, and Bob Winn—were always very supportive. Over the years, as I occasionally taught courses on comic books and historical narratives, my students have also helped me think more carefully about explaining all this. A former student, Christopher Wurpts, an artist and comics scholar in his own right, give me good advice early in my analysis of the comic strips.

Throughout the research and writing, my family was never far from my mind. My brother Steve and sister Tamara have been so happy to see this project through. My kids, Sarah and James, grew up reading these comics and talking with me about them. Sarah read an early draft of the introduction and gave me workable, incisive, and amusing advice about the organization and writing. Finally, my wife, Cheryl, has listened patiently to my rambling talk about the work, asked penetrating questions, and never flagged in her trust that I could pull this together to completion.

Clearly, I wish my mother, Patty Kugler, were still here to see this. She was thrilled I took this up and found a lot of my research not only surprising but sometimes deeply moving. I have no certain idea what my father would make of it. He would likely be mystified that his youthful drawings might interest anyone other than his family, let alone be discussed in such an extended, academic fashion. But he would possibly find the attention gratifying, this lengthy explanation fitting somehow to the hours he spent at a kitchen table ruling scrap paper with six-panel frames, eager to discover inside them his heart's desires. I dedicate this book, then, to my family.

Into the Jungle!

Introduction

> I guess I've been reading too many wild western stories and seeing too many crime pictures.
>
> —Confession of a nineteen-year-old Overton, Nebraska, man arrested for robbery, armed with six-shooters, dressed in chaps, boots, and a ten-gallon hat (*Dawson County Herald*, March 4, 1940)

The teacher moves between the desks. Was it muffled laughter that first caught her attention? Two boys toward the back huddle together. Glancing up, they quickly try to cover their desks with the assignment. Speaking quietly but hitting the consonants, the teacher repeats the question put to generation after generation of students: "What are you doing?"

Kids get in trouble in school for failing to pay attention, distracting other students, screwing around. That behavior includes doodling and sketching. The more orderly, regimented, pedagogic, "scientific" the education, perhaps the more interesting the boys' drawings. Imagine the teacher extracting the following image from the sweaty hands of those boys (fig. 1.1). Of course, the response could be outrage, amusement, or indifference. But this drawing by James William "Jimmy" Kugler (1932–1969), oddly enough, might have been his distinctive reply—even retaliation—for a particular kind of school system. It surely was a reply to a particular time and place: a small Nebraska town after the Second World War. This image is only one of a large collection of adolescent drawings concentrating first, it appears, on the War in the Pacific and then developing into stories of violence in gradually more grotesque and comic ways.[1] It responded to an adult culture moving in seemingly different directions. This art challenged the convictions behind a modern, rural school system devoted to domesticating children, using public education to instill obedient citizenship, decent morals, and personal hygiene, objectives that appeared more urgent in wartime.[2] This energetic, even progressive educational system was central to a range of organizations and programs intended to meet a "youth crisis" of growing unemployment among young people during the Depression, the problems of young people with too much free time unsupervised by their parents, and later, youth as consumers—all contributing, many claimed, to delinquency.[3]

This educational program also welcomed—too strong a word?—the national state at war. Alongside the schools, radio and newspapers and also movies and comic books freely portrayed a coordinated civic authority united with private citizens against tyranny. This struggle, conveyed in images and stories across the media, exhibited military violence justified by patriotic necessity. Appeals to national unity and cooperation, necessary to justify the brutal duty of killing an apparently numberless and relentless, merciless enemy, do not sit well with admonitions to order, decency, self-control, and respectability. But for a creative adolescent living under such invocations to patriotism, as well as insistence on moral decency, drawings depicting the dynamic thrill of fighting, even the anarchism of violence, show the student "back talking" the adults in charge.[4] There is no surprise in a kid's disrespect for his elders. But there are not many records of sustained, detailed talking back that also suggest what he's read, watched, and

Figure 1.1

heard.[5] This young man's drawings are an archive of American adolescent understanding and an interpretation of the experience of war as he received it from popular culture.

The drawings also mark the evolving dreamscape of the early popular culture of horror and the macabre into the 1950s. Despite a comic horizon filled with superheroes, Jimmy's characters exhibit neither great powers nor, for that matter, great responsibilities. His characters—he called them "Frogs" and "Toads"—behave like cartoon versions of humans. As iconic people, his characters follow the frenetic, violent trail Jimmy set for them in the "what if?" of his imagined war. Rather than achieve conformity and uniformity, for some young Americans the institutions of modern public education and mass media provoked rebellion.[6] So, imagine a small midwestern town. For some people, the bigger, faster, louder, and more interesting world was beyond. What does a war look like? What is aerial bombing like? How do you describe vengeful retaliation for it? How can you re-create, through art, the strafing of enemy troops? Or savage hand-to-hand combat? What happens in comic frames when the imagination moves from that small midwestern town to naval battles, island invasions, and jungle warfare? War and terrifying violence are the responsibilities of grownups, but children too are witnesses.[7]

"Jimmy" Kugler of Lexington, Nebraska, was twelve years old in 1944. As far as I can tell, sometime between the seventh grade and high school, he drew nearly one hundred twenty cartoon strips, almost half of which retold the War in the Pacific.[8] The archive is mostly nine-by-six-inch sheets of paper drawn only in pencil, most on both sides. Two were probably classroom doodles, drawn on mimeographed handouts of poetry and instructions for delivering a public address.[9] The archive has three main parts: "The Famous War of the Frogs and Toads" (fifty-nine sheets), which includes the stories "What Started the War," "The Fall of Frogington," "The Fate of a Toad Convoy," "The Battle of Toadajima" (unfinished), and "The Fall of Eagle Island." The second large part, "The Mystery of the Winged Frogs" (thirty-three sheets), is a gothic-noir horror story. The remainder are a range of single-frame comics, humorously violent for the most part (twenty-three sheets including "I'll teach you to step on my shadow!" or a sardonic depiction of torture conjured in "The Process of the Iron Maiden"). Finally, there are two unfinished stories, a different noir mystery and "Food Frog, in 'Who's Got the Watermelon?'" (four sheets).

The near-omnipresence of the comic book or graphic novel throughout our popular culture has inspired a great deal of sophisticated and thoughtful scholarship. We could still find ways to dismiss comic books for their crude, prurient (at best, "low") character.[10] But one of the earliest champions of this serious attention, Gilbert Seldes, caught the right tone in the early 1920s: "I am sure that a history of manners in the United States could be composed with the comic strip as its golden thread; but I think that something more than its vulgarity would be revealing."[11] The golden thread of this historical scholarship splits into two paths. One, the history of comics themselves, suggests a range of contexts that shaped the stories and art, and in turn provoked succeeding artists.[12] Another approach treats comics as historical narratives themselves, especially as biography and memoir.[13] A few scholars work along both lines of thought.[14] For Jimmy's comic strips, this historian, strangely, is the son interrogating his father's adolescent drawings. This project, like others, tries to explain the comics' origins in the complex world of American popular culture before, during, and after the war.[15] I also want to suggest what the comics tell us about the experience of war through popular media for a young American white male. Histories of modern childhood, as far as I can tell, pay little attention to the reading of and responses to the comic book among youth and adolescents.[16]

Clearly, this project combines a variety of scholarship from a range of different fields. Jimmy's comics are not autobiographical; as a "funny animal" fantasy of World War II, their narration of the war is thematically limited. Reading, watching, and looking widely into what remains of the popular culture of the 1940s, to gain some interpretive insight into the comic strips themselves, seems much more like a project in the microhistory of a boy's adolescence than other forms of comic book scholarship.[17] In this introduction, I will describe the Lexington of Jimmy's childhood in the war years. I'll then turn to the war comics themselves, outlining their settings and storyline. I'll follow that with an overview of Jimmy's depiction of combat in the air, at sea, and on land. Then, I'll provide a broad cultural context for the comics from comic books and strips as well as movies, radio, newspaper, and propaganda images. I hope I can suggest a wide and rich treasury of popular media Jimmy drew on to build his unusual, dynamic and violent retelling of the war.

The story about that boy and his drawings starts in Lexington, Nebraska.[18]

Growing Up in Wartime, Small-Town Nebraska

The second-largest town in Dawson County with a 1940 population of over thirty-six hundred, Lexington was a railroad hub and county seat near the Platte River, surrounded by beets, alfalfa, grass, corn, and livestock yards.[19] Throughout the 1930s, the *Lexington Clipper* promoted its attractions and opportunities, while expressing the residents' fears and anxieties specific to small towns.[20] A Roosevelt White House enjoyed limited local confidence,[21] and the paper regularly reported worries about foreclosures and business closures in the city and county. Re-armament brought employment, while editorials criticized unions and strikes.[22]

In the summer, the *Clipper* registered local anxiety about grasshoppers and storms; in the fall, it returned to local high school grads attending Nebraska colleges and apprehension about the brain drain. Both the *Clipper* and the *Dawson County Herald* reported the minor tragedies of farm accidents, explosions, train crossing deaths, auto collisions on rural roads, vandalism, thefts, and fights. For reassurance, the paper and official media organs boosted Lexington for its reputation across Nebraska as the "greatest little city in the country."[23]

Entertainment and spectacle, homegrown or gifts from the wide world, helped ease stress. The biggest yearly event, Plum Creek Days held in late May, commemorated the pioneer settlement of the area. Residents attended car and motorcycle stunt-driving shows. At the Armory, residents celebrated Mexican Independence Day. The Dawson County fair and rodeo in late August brought people from around the area. High school sports and summer semi-pro baseball were popular. Each fall, costumed children joined the town Halloween parade. For the pious, First Presbyterian Church (which at twelve, Jimmy joined) held regular synods in Lexington featuring respected seminary professors and missionaries. Celebrities like Gracie Allen and George Burns made headlines when their train stopped in town.[24]

Joseph Amato suggested that some of the most significant parts of local history are hidden inside an invisible community.[25] Some of this might be gleaned from the local papers, through which reporters shone a light on Lexington's seamier side. A big murder trial could magnetize the community, as in the fall of 1939. Prominent farmer and stockman Herbert Malm was assassinated by his brother-in-law. The front page reported a standing-room-only trial, depicted how the killer first wounded Malm with a shotgun, switching to a pistol to shoot him twice in the head.[26] Occasionally the only reasonable response was uncomfortable laughter, intentional or not. The July 21, 1938 *Clipper* reported that the previous Saturday a thirteen-year-old boy drowned at Lexington's public pool. Immediately below that read "Water Safety School Started Wednesday." The *Clipper*'s regular column of humor and local news, "Ink Spots!," reported on September 21, 1939, the death of resident "Miles Maryott, 87, the 'artist-slayer.'" Paroled the previous May for murdering a policeman, he was apparently as skilled with a pencil as he was with a handgun. For a town where fat-rendering trucks promised "Dead Stock Removed Free" and "our trucks are steam cleaned and disinfected daily," and where the front page included the county corn-husking contest winners (*Clipper*, October 21, 1937; October 28, 1937), the sensational and the darkly humorous often accompanied the routine.

As in most places, the war changed Lexington. In the year or so leading up to Pearl Harbor, local papers ran regular editorials opposing American intervention, while the pages were lined with advertisements depicting military vehicles, accounts of Japanese aggression in Asia, and stories and letters on locals serving in the military. In June 1941, during Plum Creek Days, the *Clipper* and *Herald* ran photos of a Lexington man dressed as a Greek soldier with a rifle chasing someone dressed as Mussolini. Almost four months before the US entered the war, the *Clipper* reported the brief visit of a freight train carrying one of the largest artillery pieces built for the US military. The author touted the gun's remarkable size and power and the well-armed soldiers guarding it, speculating that it was due west to defend America's coast.[27] During the war, the paper reported local men and women serving, the difficulty of keeping public school teachers from enlisting or leaving for better-paying jobs at defense plants, and editorials chastising slack local sales of war bonds.[28] Of course, Nebraskans worried about their loved ones in uniform; over three thousand residents died serving their country.[29] German POWs were held in the state, and some of the camps were near Lexington.[30] Nebraska had several Army Air Corps bases and young pilots regularly trained overhead in fighters and bombers.[31] Surrounded by a cloud of apprehension, evangelists offered big public prophecy seminars suggesting contemporary signs of the End Times, the appearance of the Antichrist in the rise of totalitarian dictators, and spiritual reassurance before mobilized armies of biblical proportions.[32]

Small-town papers, typically, boost an area's livability, investment prospects, and the celebration of residents' accomplishments. I don't want to suggest that Lexington's papers offered a clear or neutral look into the regional affairs of the 1940s. It is also difficult to know anything about readership. But the paper can give us some sense of what townspeople considered significant, even noteworthy. What's more, Jimmy Kugler's dad worked as a typesetter or "operator" for Lexington's *Clipper*.[33] While the paper selected and filtered the local and world affairs for its audience, Jimmy might have had special access to the paper. But that was not his only, or even primary, perspective on Lexington. Long before the war, Dawson County seemed full of Kuglers. In Lexington, the men typically worked as blacksmiths or on road crews, while those outside farmed and operated feed lots.

Jimmy's father, Otto Carl Kugler, was the son of German immigrants. Otto's father William [Wilhelm] had been a blacksmith. Jimmy's immigrant grandmother, Marie, William's second wife, never learned to speak much English.[34] During the Great War, Otto served in Omaha; in 1928 he married Daisy Hamilton of Plattsmouth. Along with many other Lexington men in the 1920s, he joined the Ku Klux Klan.[35] Through the 1940s, Jimmy moved around a good deal, living in at least four different cramped houses, probably occasionally living with his grandmother in her small Lexington home.[36] Fortunately, Otto stayed employed through the Depression.

The adult Jim remembered an unhappy childhood. He was the only child born to a forty-year-old man and a woman eight years younger. Otto and Daisy drank; Otto so much that sometime during Jimmy's childhood, the *Clipper* might have sent him away to an Omaha hospital to dry out.[37] Daisy was a hairdresser at the Modern Beauty Shop

Figure 1.2 Marie Kugler's home (Jimmy's residence from 1941 to 1948).

where Jimmy swept the floor after school.[38] The couple had troubles; Daisy walked out. They divorced sometime in Jimmy's boyhood, possibly in 1945/6.[39] He was raised mostly by his father and on occasion by Marie, who died in 1941 when he was nine. He recalled often being alone at night. Returning from watching a horror movie at one of the theaters, he claimed he was so frightened in the dark, empty house made eerie by the wind and trees scratching at the windows that he would grab the kitchen knives and lay them on the table next to his bed. These tiny houses still stand, mute to a boy's life alone with an alcoholic father in his fifties (fig. 1.2).

None of Jimmy's contemporaries from those days in Lexington remembered if his childhood was happy or unhappy (fig. 1.3). He played basketball and football into high school. His West Ward grade school reported that he was a good student. He averaged high "B" and

Second row: Coach Grote, O. Reiker, J. Mallett, R. Bredenkamp, W. Owens, J. Young, E. Kirwan, J. Randecker.
First row: J. Reynolds, G. Kreitz, L. Phillippi, J. Kugler, R. Brown, B. McKee, B. Aten.

Figure 1.3 Jimmy Kugler (#7) on the junior high school basketball team (Lexington High School yearbook, *The Minuteman*, 1948). Courtesy of Dawson County Historical Museum.

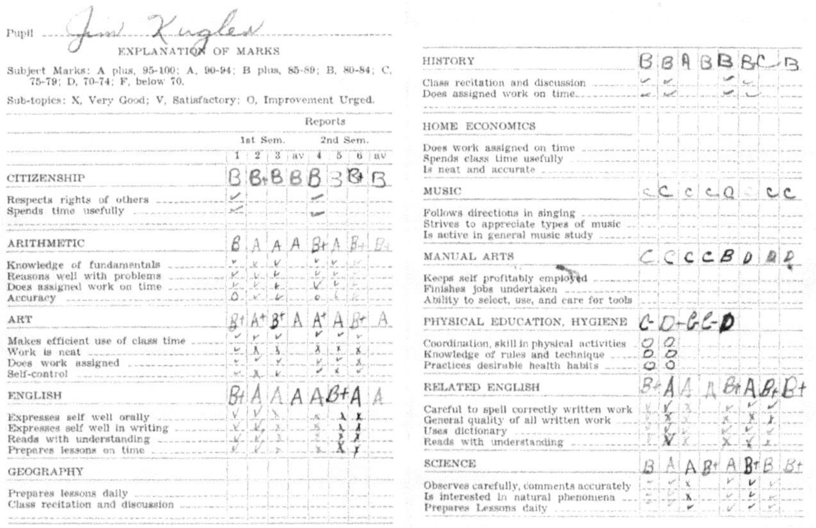

Pupil Jim Kugler

EXPLANATION OF MARKS

Subject Marks: A plus, 95-100; A, 90-94; B plus, 85-89; B, 80-84; C, 75-79; D, 70-74; F, below 70.

Sub-topics: X, Very Good; V, Satisfactory; O, Improvement Urged.

	Reports							
	1st Sem.				2nd Sem.			
	1	2	3	av	4	5	6	av
CITIZENSHIP	B	B+	B	B	B	B	B+	B
Respects rights of others	✓				✓			
Spends time usefully	✓				✓			
ARITHMETIC	B	A	A	A	B+	A	B+	B+
Knowledge of fundamentals	✓	✓	✓		✓	✓	✓	
Reasons well with problems	✓	✓	✓		✓	✓	✓	
Does assigned work on time	✓	✓	✓		✓	✓	✓	
Accuracy	O	✓	✓		O	✓	✓	
ART	B+	A+	B+	A	A+	A	B+	A
Makes efficient use of class time	✓	✓	✓		✓	✓	✓	
Work is neat	✓	X	X		X	X	X	
Does work assigned	✓	✓	✓		✓	✓	X	
Self-control	✓	X	✓		✓	✓	✓	
ENGLISH	B+	A	A	A	A	B+	A	A
Expresses self well orally	✓	✓	X		X	X	X	
Expresses self well in writing	✓	✓	X		X	X	X	
Reads with understanding	✓	✓	X		X	X	X	
Prepares lessons on time	✓	✓	X		X	X	X	
GEOGRAPHY								
Prepares lessons daily								
Class recitation and discussion								
HISTORY	B	B	A	B	B	B	C-	B
Class recitation and discussion	✓	✓			✓	✓		
Does assigned work on time	✓	✓			✓	✓		
HOME ECONOMICS								
Does work assigned on time								
Spends class time usefully								
Is neat and accurate								
MUSIC	C	C	C	C	C	[illegible]	C	C
Follows directions in singing								
Strives to appreciate types of music								
Is active in general music study								
MANUAL ARTS	C	C	C	C	B	D	D	D
Keeps self profitably employed								
Finishes jobs undertaken								
Ability to select, use, and care for tools								
PHYSICAL EDUCATION, HYGIENE	C-	D-	C	C-	D			
Coordination, skill in physical activities	O	O						
Knowledge of rules and technique	O	O						
Practices desirable health habits	O	O						
RELATED ENGLISH	B+	A	A	A	B+	A	B+	B+
Careful to spell correctly written work	✓	✓	X		✓	✓	✓	
General quality of all written work	X	X	X		X	X	X	
Uses dictionary	✓	✓	✓		✓	✓	✓	
Reads with understanding	✓	X	X		X	✓	X	
SCIENCE	B	A	A	B+	A	B+	B	B+
Observes carefully, comments accurately	✓	✓	X		✓	✓	✓	
Is interested in natural phenomena	✓	✓	X		✓	✓	✓	
Prepares Lessons daily		✓	✓		✓	✓	✓	

Figure 1.4 Jimmy's eighth-grade report card, 1945–46.

"A" grades through his sophomore year in high school (fig. 1.4). He was particularly good at writing, reading, math, and art. However, he was not so great in music, PE, and hygiene. On his eighth-grade report card, his teacher marked the statement "practices desirable health habits" with "improvement urged."

Difficult as his home life appears, his parents were likely proud of his school work. Class reports published in the *Clipper* support this.[40] Jimmy's name regularly appears from the first grade through the eighth grade for reading aloud, spelling, writing, and art. He was often one of the kids selected to draw seasonal blackboard decorations for Halloween, Christmas, or Easter. He had various hobbies, his teachers reported, bringing to class his collections of Native American artifacts, rocks, and scrapbooks. The class news also reported his drawing for class projects on Africa, Holland, and prehistoric humans.[41]

The Adolescent Imagination and Movies, Comic Books, Papers, and Radio

Jimmy was a fourth grader when Japan attacked Pearl Harbor. Americans followed the news of the war through various media, but only after it had been carefully shaped and censored according to guidelines set by the Office of War Information (OWI) founded in June of 1942. It is hard to distinguish some of that coverage from propaganda. Determined to restrict rather than manipulate evidence, President Franklin D. Roosevelt oversaw a complex bureaucracy of image production and guidelines, a system never really marked by a single central authority, let alone a shared set of censorship procedures. Alongside the OWI was the Office of Censorship, and the Bureau of Public Relations in the Department of War, under Secretary Harry L. Stimson with Nelson Rockefeller as Coordinator of Inter-American

Affairs. Each branch of the military oversaw the credentialing of reporters and setting boundaries for media access to combat. Coordinating all of these was unworkable, nor was it possible to oversee the daily broadcasts of hundreds of radio stations and newspapers throughout the country. It appears that independent media outlets, for the most part, policed themselves. They shared, as George Roeder suggested, a "way of seeing war."[42] Yet for them, as well as the government itself, oversight of war information and images was often guided by a sincere concern to inform the American people while protecting military secrets as well as the families and friends of those serving in combat. Roosevelt recognized that the appearance of candor, if not on occasion its reality, was necessary to maintain public trust and morale. Tell the truth; just not the entire truth.[43]

In the end, public morale—support for the war effort, and practically speaking, working faithfully in war industries and buying war bonds—was the single greatest concern of the OWI head Wilmer Davis, of Secretary of Treasury Henry Morgenthau Jr., and many others intimately involved in the domestic information side of the war effort. This concern stood out as Allied forces in the Pacific experienced an almost unbroken string of defeats and setbacks throughout most of 1942. As American forces in 1943 began winning naval battles and bloody footholds on one Pacific island after another, Roosevelt, Morgenthau, Davis, and other key figures in the administration and domestic military grew concerned that American morale would shift to overconfidence and complacency. General Marshall especially considered it necessary to put in front of the public far more realistic, brutal evidence of the human cost of war. Officials were shockingly blunt in their hope that images of US casualties, especially following the invasion of Italy in early September 1943, would anger the American public and push even higher bond sales.[44]

As the Pacific War in particular developed into an inevitable air campaign against the island of Japan itself, public support as a form of domestic service parallel to that of the military was clearly the message of nearly every war bond drive. That support could not waver in the face of obvious sympathy for Japanese civilian deaths, let alone the distinction between the leaders of Imperial Japan's military—depicted in propaganda as cunning, treacherous, and savagely implacable—and the average Japanese serviceman. Images of dead GIs, which began appearing in earnest in papers and bond ads in late 1943, had to suggest a kind of reverence or dignity in a noble death. Quite differently, depictions of the Japanese war dead could be far more vivid and disturbing, suggesting an entirely deserving end to the "savage" individual's role in an undifferentiated Imperial war machine.[45] While US forces steamed into the Pacific Theater, Lexington's grade school curriculum tracked the course of the war in geography and history. Like many American kids, Jimmy participated in scrap and war savings stamp drives to raise money for military equipment.[46] Some of his distant relatives apparently served. How else might a kid like him have followed the war? With the news, did he find inspiration from other comic strips?

The *Lexington Clipper* and *Dawson County Herald* did not carry syndicated cartoon strips other than specifically patriotic propaganda. Any comics Jimmy read must have been primarily in syndicated strips from papers his father brought home and comic books. Jimmy had some Big Little Books, reprints of syndicated strips collected into small, thick book form that included some written narrative. He had a couple of *Mickey Mouse* and *Alley Oop* versions.[47] Among his personal items is a comic page from Salt Lake City's *Deseret News* dated June 13, 1940, after Jimmy had completed the second grade. The comics take up an entire page and include such famous strips as *Li'l Abner*,

Figure 1.5

The Lone Ranger, and *Tarzan*, and obscure ones like Les Forgrave's *Big Sister* and John Millar Watt's *Pop*. The survival of this part of a city paper from Jimmy's childhood is a relic from a time when newspaper staffers subscribed to other papers whose editorials regularly appeared in the *Clipper*. Having a son who could read at an early age and was also interested in drawing cartoons, Jimmy's father could easily have brought home the comics from any number of papers as near as Omaha or far away as the West Coast (fig. 1.5).

Jimmy was not only reading comics. Long before the war, radio, movies, and toys captured the attention, and spare change, of American children. A variety of marketing campaigns targeting children accelerated in the 1930s. Corporations responded to an increasingly idealized childhood characterized by the necessity of free time for creative play designed to encourage young imaginations. Toy companies associated their products directly with radio and film programs, often based on cartoon animal characters.[48] Radio and serialized pulp fiction were very popular with kids and adults. As an adult, Jimmy related how he followed radio mysteries like *The Whistler* and *The Shadow*.[49] Once the war began, national radio coverage was extensive; in the first year following Pearl Harbor, a whole range of often melodramatic shows on everything from combat news to portraits of fascism to scrap drives and nutrition contributed significantly to the public sense of what "total war" would ask of civilians.[50]

Mass media typically illustrated the American cause as entirely devoted to protecting liberty and democracy in a world-wide war against savage, totalitarian enemies.[51] During the war, Hollywood produced movies to conform to OWI guidelines. These, too, seem to have filled Jimmy's imagination. It would be no surprise if he spent a lot of his free time at the town's two theaters, the Majestic and the Ralf, since his parents often left him alone (fig. 1.6).[52] In 1938, you could see a movie in Lexington for as little as fifteen cents. The local papers advertised comedies, dramas, and Westerns until just before the war, everything from *Gone with the Wind* to *Tarzan*. In February 1941, *Flight Command* opened at the Majestic, and other war films followed.[53] After Pearl Harbor, Hollywood poured them out. The ads appearing in the *Clipper* were dynamic. For August 26, 1943, the Majestic spot for *Hitler's Madmen* ("The Stark Story of the Rape of Lidice") shows a woman kneeling before a whip-wielding Nazi officer, her clothes slipping from her shoulder. "Captive women sentenced to a living death . . . the firing squad for all men . . . foul concentration camps for children!"

On September 16, 1943, the paper announced *Behind the Rising Sun* for the Midwest premier, challenging patrons to "see why the

Figure 1.6 Outside the Majestic Theater, Lexington, ca. 1950. Courtesy of Dawson County Historical Museum.

villainous Jap war lords have got to be EXTERMINATED!" In the center a hulking Japanese soldier with shadowed face, bright eyes and teeth—nearly as monstrous as any character from the comic books—leans over a helpless woman in a negligee (the hulking figure is recalled in the pose of the Frog transformed into a Toad; see figure 1.17). In the background, another soldier beats a bound man. Below the film title reads, "The sensational picture that shows the 'Sons of Heaven' at their 'honorable' duties of torture, treachery and carnage . . . harsh truths that will make you recoil with shocked amazement

Figure 1.7 War as horror, the enemy as monsters: movie ad from the *Lexington Clipper*, September 16, 1943.

as you boil with fighting anger!" How many films promise you'll boil and recoil at the same time? (fig. 1.7).[54]

Horror films gradually crept onto Lexington screens; the first in four years, *Dr. Jekyll and Mr. Hyde*, was advertised in November 1941. On August 5, 1943, *I Walked with a Zombie* played; the ad includes a creepy image of a darkened woman's face, glowing eyes, hands groping toward the reader. The March 16, 1944 ad for the Jack the Ripper film *The Lodger* added a "Warning!" with a dagger for an exclamation mark. "Be sure to bring someone along with you when you see . . . *The Lodger*." This invitation to the "sensational story of crime's most vicious killer!" is followed by a sinister promise: "I'm at the Majestic Theater, Lexington, this Thursday-Friday-Saturday, March 16–17–18 with my thrills-chills, etc., etc., —signed, JACK THE RIPPER." A May 11, 1944 ad for the classic *The Uninvited* promised "Evil Incarnate . . . a spirit of supreme malignance . . . threatened him . . . hating the living." Imagine a boy like Jimmy, his mind roiled by such movies, returning in the dark to an empty house.

By 1945, the American taste for the war film waned. Horror and suspense films endured, while romances, musicals, dramas, and Westerns returned to local screens. Readership in superhero and war comics declined at about the same time.[55] Considering the movies as well as the advertisements for them, a boy who read the papers and their graphic reports of local death and maiming, who kept up on the war as well as other adventure fiction in radio and print, was ripe with imagined mayhem and spine-scraping storytelling. *Behind the Rising Sun* promised Japanese soldiers who easily looked like the monsters of horror films and comic books.

Jimmy's war comics suggest a faint trail of other possible influences. He probably knew of the Army Air Corps bases in Nebraska, and might have seen training flights in the skies above Lexington (see note 31). The *Clipper* reported that he had been drawing airplanes since he was small. Three months before Pearl Harbor, the nine-year-old boy had shown his classmates his scrapbook of airplane art. No surprise; after Pearl Harbor, the *Clipper* included many images of fighters, bombers, aircraft carriers, and other military equipment and soldiers.[56] The war in words and images, especially for war bond ads, dominated America's local papers.[57] Most ads were dramatic, vivid, and cinematic. Usually sentimentally patriotic, occasionally slapstick, they grew grimmer and more strident as the war wore on, and the Treasury Department worried that public exhaustion with the war would lead to slack bond sales. James Kimble depicts the war bond campaigns as evidence that propaganda programs encouraged the "militarization" of America's civic life. The Fourth and Fifth campaigns especially depicted the grave situation facing American troops against a savage, inhuman Japanese enemy. These harsh images were often coupled with depictions of American families at home, terrorized by an occupying enemy should US forces suffer defeat.[58]

These campaigns made no effort to shelter children from their grim purposes. The Third War Bond (September 1943) inaugurated the Schools at War program, recruiting children for door-to-door sales campaigns as well as buying bonds themselves. This further conflated military service with civilian service at home. Kimble concluded his study by suggesting that the bond campaigns had the unintended consequence of inuring the public to the horrors and suffering of war and dehumanizing the Japanese deserving destruction, yet were strangely acceptable when sanitized in the light of the "perfecting" cause of democracy and national security.[59]

The ads often exploited stereotypes of the Japanese as relentless murderers in a kill-or-be-killed struggle. Some relied on sobering portraits of dead soldiers. Others touched the poetic in gothic conventions. Artists could readily appeal to the most disturbing audience fears: "This isn't war . . . it's murder!"[60] Some of the ads appearing in the *Clipper* rivaled the most exciting and shocking violence to be seen on screen or in horror comics (fig. 1.8).[61] But just in case an image this graphic is misunderstood, the ad reads, "'That's the way I like to see them,' said Gen. MacArthur when he saw the rows of dead Japs in the Admiralty Islands." A war of "savage fury" demands public support to defeat "the most treacherous forces Americans have ever met in combat." Such exposition hardly needed the image of an American soldier bayonetting an enemy who is a split second away from stabbing him to death. Interestingly, a German soldier illustrates the treachery and savagery of Japanese troops who, MacArthur stated, must be killed to be defeated.[62]

A bright kid who could read from an early age was also an only child left to his own devices in a broken home. Able to spend hours of dedicated perseverance necessary to draw dozens of cartoon frames and keeping scrapbooks of airplane images, Jimmy was surely capable of reading the local papers. He apparently had the free time alone to brood over the news in radio and newspapers, from movies and comics, all dedicated to covering the war and inspiring patriotic support.[63] The *Clipper* reported the Pacific War with Japan more than the European Theater; perhaps Pearl Harbor made Japan a closer, deeper threat than the war against Hitler.[64] Americans had fought in the Pacific Theater for over two years before meeting Germany on the European continent. Until well after D-Day, the grinding brutality of the island war of the Pacific and the cruelty of combat against the Japanese were more fully reported by journalists than the European campaign.[65]

War as adventure came to American youth long before Pearl Harbor. For some time, manufacturers targeted American boys with military toys. By the 1930s, advertising for toys and films directly linked young male fantasies toward warfare. War toys marketed to

Figure 1.8 The Germano-Japanese Enemy: Ad for the Fifth War Bond, *Lexington Clipper*, June 22, 1944.

boys had taken off.[66] The violence of boys' play and the anarchistic character of adolescent culture mirrored the images of deadly adventure and titillating mayhem in the films, film ads, and comic books of the war years. Media portrayals of the war as virtuous self-defense and justified vengeance made mayhem legitimate in ways adolescents could easily have noticed.[67]

The war fought in mass-marketed mainstream comics was not exceptional. As I suggested earlier, most people recognized the power of comic books, for good or ill, and American creators of wartime propaganda eagerly exploited public taste for cartoons. Early in the conflict, the OWI each week sent four war-related cartoons to around eight hundred US newspapers; funding limits later ended this.[68] Milton Caniff's *Terry and the Pirates* was as sympathetic and nuanced toward the Far East as any strip drawn during the war, yet the artist suggested the eerie otherworldliness and racial stereotypes of a largely uniform Asian civilization, whether it was from Burma, China, or Japan.[69] Like Caniff, the local papers, and films, Jimmy included his own maps in the war comics to help orient the reader and to give them a factual, official air. Far uglier were the portraits of Japanese in comic books like *Airboy* and *Captain Midnight*. *Air Fighters Comics*, beginning in 1941, was dominated by Japanese characters speaking Pidgin English with prominent teeth and the slanted eyes of a rodent.[70] Often, the Japanese look like monkeys.[71] Japanese leaders were monstrous, armed with knobby, clawed hands, fanged teeth, and even scales.[72] They kill without remorse; they torture with sadistic joy; they happily betray the "white men" they hate with racist fanaticism.[73]

What did the war do for Jimmy's art? Among the obvious, the war unlocked a set of desires for what he wanted to look at, to witness, in the act of creating. He wanted to see the war, but on his own terms. He wanted to see it up close, selected for the aspects of the war that fascinated him, and how those aspects, revised and re-created by him, let him both see and feel in a deeply personal way the intimacy of creation as immediate experience.[74] As one classmate recalled from Lexington High School, Jimmy and Jack Kutz (class of 1950) handed the comics around to their male classmates. In doing so, Jimmy may well have ramped up the violence, the cruelty, for further kudos among his peers.[75] Still, from the start, he made clear his tastes in a certain kind of conflict and its depiction. If an audience egged him on to greater extremes, he readily matched their enthusiasm. All told, Jimmy built the comics from elements supplied by the popular culture surrounding the war, mediated in various ways in small-town Lexington. Comic books have a popular reputation for encouraging adolescent tastes for crude violence, largely in the terms of Fredric Wertham's notorious 1954 *Seduction of the Innocent*: "Now no holds are barred. Horror, crime, sadism, monsters, ghouls, corpses dead and alive—in short, real freedom of expression. All this in comic books addressed to and sold to children."[76] Looking at Jimmy's war comics, we find his inspirations not only throughout popular culture, but encouraged by American wartime propaganda. He chose what he may or may not have put into words: retelling the war to himself in new ways.[77]

The War Comics

In his history of combat experience in the Civil War, author Gerald Linderman suggested, "Every war begins as one war and becomes two, that watched by civilians, and that fought by soldiers."[78] Perhaps a third kind of war emerges from the first: the war retold. Sketched in pencil, Jimmy's war comic strips do not initially suggest singular artwork. He represented characters in profile, occasionally the front of the face and body. His characters, bipedal "Frogs," are idealized; at first glance, simple. This, of course, was not unusual. Comic strips of the period—*Dick Tracy*, *Terry and the Pirates*, *Alley Oop*—were instantly recognizable for the profiles of the main characters. Jimmy would occasionally use cinematic perspectives like close-ups or long distance—the "God's eye view"—especially in the war comics. But they have no odd perspectives or adventurous cinematic views. There was certainly nothing in them like the vibrantly three-dimensional action of Jack Kirby's *Captain America* or Burne Hogarth's *Tarzan* of the early 1940s. Jimmy's war comics borrowed framing and elements from newsreels and combat films: shots from bombers above a target, of planes strafing ships, of sailors firing on a beach, and, often, of hand-to-hand combat. When drawing ships, tanks, and planes, he also concentrated on the profile. Typically, his ships were shaded silhouettes that conveyed form without the photorealistic detail common to that era's combat movies and comic books.[79]

Jimmy's cartoon storytelling left behind a sizeable archive reflecting the work of a dedicated artist and storyteller. It is a rich artifact of a boy's imagination filtering his experience of popular culture and mass media immediately after wartime, perhaps for a few years later. His war comics followed the general storyline of the origins of the US entering the Second World War. What fear and excitement from a Japanese air attack had haunted American children? What had they seen of reports of German aerial attacks on Poland, France, or Great Britain? Children recounted daydreams and nightmares of Japanese or German tanks and planes attacking their towns. Young residents of midwestern towns, far inland, told of similar fears. Wartime propaganda often depicted children frightened of the invading German troops, wearing gas masks, or looking forward to the day when the sound of an airplane overhead was not a source of dread.[80] Comic books regularly had covers with German U-boats, tanks, or bombers attacking Washington, DC. Before Pearl Harbor, the superhero Steel

Sterling appeared on the cover of *Zip Comics* struggling against a Nazi Grim Reaper, while New York City burned in the foreground. Comic covers often promised stories of spies, saboteurs and fifth-column men attacking American dams, reservoirs, or factories.[81] In many wartime comic books, the superhero in combat invited young readers to imagine themselves fighting alongside the adult, famously so when Bucky teamed with Captain America.[82] These kinds of stories and images meshed quite well with war bond ads inviting children to imagine themselves "fighting" alongside GIs by "serving" in the Boy Scouts or school contests to "buy" a tank or bomber.[83]

Jimmy drew his own version of the initial surprise air raid on "Frogtown." Violating a sunny Sabbath and day off, pilots of a cruel regime unjustly bomb and strafe peaceful civilians (pages 67–72).[84] The Toad air force even targets women and children—the only two frames depicting women or youth in all his comics. Jimmy's imagined atrocity is not too far from the standard comic and illustrated depictions of the Japanese and Germans in his local papers, where ads for films, bond sales, and editorial cartoons trafficked in typical images.[85] "Atrocity" stories and pictures often characterized coverage of both Japanese and German soldiers. Several years before Pearl Harbor, the Luftwaffe had bombed and strafed cities throughout Spain, Poland, France, Great Britain, and Russia without discriminating between soldiers and civilians. Occasionally, these reports and the accompanying images were quite violent. Yet, they were heavily and carefully censored. Reporting in various forms could assert, too, that the enemy, especially the Japanese, were little more than animals. Such images meant that the Japanese and Germans, unlike the Allies, did not live normal lives nor were they moved by compassion. The Toads' sneak attack targeted churches, libraries, civilians, apartments, nonmilitary airfields—the idealized infrastructure of a modern, peaceful democratic society.

Jimmy's consistent narrative tactic was to waste little or no time on exposition or context. The war begins viciously, apparently unprovoked. He gave no portrait of Toads debating going to war. It just erupts as an apocalypse from the sky. Jimmy's Toads were the natural expression of a militarized collective.

Toad treachery and cruelty were simply their nature. We never see the Toads in their native land; no Toad families or scenes of leisure. "The Fate of a Toad Convoy" begins briefly on the Toad mainland, but nothing else suggests their character or the peculiarities of their region. Such information is not important; it only matters that they are cunning, brutal adversaries. Their ripsaw teeth and sinister eyes capture all the viewer needs to know about their intentions and character (page 123).

Once Jimmy's war begins, it is not clear which chapter follows which. The introduction admits that the Frogs "did not have time to put men on all their islands before the toads landed." It suggests that the next chapter is "The Fall of Frogington," which begins by explaining how little time the Frogs have to bolster their defenses against another Toad raid. "The Fate of a Toad Convoy" perhaps comes next; the commander explains to his aide that the convoy must establish a base on Eagle Island, from which they can launch their assault on Frogville. Whatever the order, this will be the only Frog victory; "Frogington" and "Eagle Island" are Toad triumphs. Of the four chapters, only "The Fall of Frogington" and "The Battle of Toadajima" have their own splash title pages. There's no mention of a Frog "mainland" as there is for the Toads. There's a logic to Jimmy's distinction. If Frogs are amphibious, it makes sense that they live on islands. Toads, resembling Frogs but not water-loving creatures, would be primarily land-going. Does this make the Frog-US/Toad-Japan parallel even less obvious? We see much more of the Frog world, providing some background, than we do of the Toads'. The reader's sympathies are moved to favor the Frogs, their aggrieved status as victims, and their just desire for revenge.

"The Fall of Frogington" seems an early installment in Jimmy's war saga. His artwork does not seem as accomplished as that of other chapters. Early exposition in "The Battle of Toadajima" states that this Toad island base has to be captured in order to make victory on "Eagle Island" and other Toad islands possible.[86] But "The Fall of Eagle Island" begins with a Toad attack on Frog forces, suggesting that, by this point in the story, the Frogs had been victorious in an earlier invasion. In the Pacific Theater, air strikes against key targets were possible only from strategic island bases. The Japanese had hoped to take Midway for such purposes against Hawaii; the US could attack the island of Japan consistently only after taking the Mariana Islands in the summer of 1944. The Toads are victorious and take the island; perhaps following this, the Frogs retake the island? It is not clear. As "The Fate of a Toad Convoy" begins, is Frogville on Eagle Island? If so, this would help explain the Toads' aerial attack on the Frogs defending Eagle Island. Or is Frogville near Eagle Island, the Toad attack making it possible to stage an assault from there? Clearly, the geography and chronology of Jimmy's war are not clear.

But Jimmy certainly had no trouble imagining the kind of place where a war he longed to narrate and see began. He reimagined a surprise attack starting in a town like Lexington. (figs. 1.9–1.13). He must have been familiar with some of these buildings, places he surely visited, even knew quite well. They are civilized, necessary landmarks of modern life. Other buildings probably enjoyed a similar status. Even beyond the war comics, Jimmy made visual references to the buildings of his hometown. He could have chosen a major city for his war, filled with skyscrapers, car-lined streets, and crowded with

Figure 1.9 Lexington's Carnegie Library, postcard from the 1950s. Courtesy of Dawson County Historical Museum.

Figure 1.10 Detail from "How the War Started."

Figure 1.11 The Cornland Hotel (razed in 1963). Courtesy of Dawson County Historical Museum.

Figure 1.12 The Dawson County Bank, now the Dan Grafton Building. Courtesy of Dawson County Historical Museum.

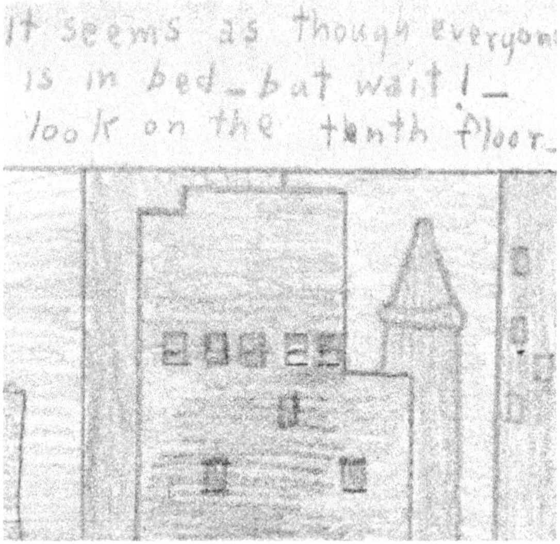
It seems as though everyon
is in bed_but wait!_
look on the tenth floor_

Figure 1.13 Detail from an untitled, unfinished story.

citizens. As the above image implies, he did set some stories in the urban canyons of Hollywood's crime mysteries and Batman comics, and some of his war comics take place in the jungles of ocean islands, far from the Nebraska plains. But Jimmy began his war in a much smaller, more intimate place. He seemed to enjoy depicting shock at the mayhem of invasion in a setting quite like that of his hometown.[87]

While American children in the war years likely absorbed some of the anxiety radiating from their parents and the news, Jimmy found an outlet for that excitement. He wondered how a typical, bright Sunday morning in Lexington could be split open by the snarl of propellers, the ratcheting wail of dive bombers, and the percussive dread of approaching machine-gun fire and explosions.

"Aheee!": Depicting Combat Above and Below

At the start of the story, the (apparently) innocent, hard-working Frogs respond with grit and dedication. Rebuilding their destroyed town, they arm and train for the looming war—the handful of frames implying that their work ethic is relentless—finally declaring war on the Toads. Perhaps to keep the distinction between Frog and Toad clear, the former soldiers wear helmets from the World War I era and are still in use early in the Pacific Theater. These M1917 helmets (similar to the British "Brodie" version) stand out in John Ford's *The Battle of Midway* and an early, key war film, Tay Garnett's 1943 *Bataan*.[88] The Frogs, in some ways, suggest the ideal civil society as Americans were depicted in war bond propaganda. Unbroken in spirit, united at home and in combat, the Frogs, however, give no rousing patriotic speeches—in fact, they say little at all about the war's meaning or purpose. This is consistent, again, with Jimmy's eagerness to get to the excitement of combat at sea and on jungle islands.[89] But it also has the effect of suggesting how the Frogs have little need to recruit one another, encourage one another, or recall one another to their duty. Their motives and "worldview," if you will, are hardly better explained or illustrated than those of the Toads.

With one exception—"The Fate of a Toad Convoy"—all the battles recount the defeat of brave but greatly outnumbered Frogs.[90] This largely follows the first year or so of American fighting against the Japanese, *if* the US = the Frog forces. After the Pearl Harbor attack, Guam and then Wake Island fell to the Japanese. In April 1942, the loss of Bataan meant the surrender of almost eighty thousand US troops. That May, around fifteen thousand US soldiers surrendered on Corregidor Island. The battle of the Java Sea was a defeat; the victory at the Coral Sea, terribly costly.[91] The first significant victory by US naval forces came in June at Midway, where greatly outnumbered Americans attacked a Japanese invasion flotilla, forcing their retreat. By the late fall of 1942, a battle opened on Guadalcanal that would last six bloody months. A year later, when Marines took Tarawa, the course of the war had shifted decisively. With this all-too-brief outline in mind, Jimmy's imaginative retelling of the Pacific Theater seems to cover roughly the war's first year.

Jimmy drew extended aerial duels between Frog and Toad pilots, imitating similar images in the air combat films of the time as well as comic books like *Air Fighters Comics* and *Captain Midnight*. Frog pilots steer crippled planes into those of their Toad rivals, re-creating mid-air collisions seen in *Flying Tigers* (David Miller, 1942) and on several covers of *Wings Comics*.[92] In one portion of "The Fall of Frogington," Jimmy depicts a Frog pilot parachuting from his burning fighter, only to be cruelly strafed by a Toad pilot (pages 82–83). The Frog pilot not only avenges his murdered comrade, but he also covers the act with black humor.[93] Often the Frog pilots, as in a key scene in

Flying Tigers, face markedly superior numbers of Toad fighters. That film was loosely based on the American Volunteer Group training in China before Pearl Harbor. Led by retired pilot Claire Lee Chennault, the group became famous for a successful Christmas Day assault over Rangoon against a superior Japanese force.[94] Caniff's *Terry and the Pirates*, in cartoon and radio versions, followed Terry into the Army Air Corps and the Flying Tigers themselves. In "The Battle of Toadajima" and "The Fall of Eagle Island," lone Frog airmen or soldiers hold off entire Toad platoons. Overwhelmed, the Frogs die bravely, fighting with cruel cunning to the end. Jimmy highlighted courageous Frogs defending their country and themselves against the relentless brute force of the massed Toad war machine.[95] Brave individual soldiers fought for survival and vengeance against an undifferentiated, modern, militaristic enemy eager to bring destruction, chaos, and suffering.

During the war, Hollywood combat movies were typically marked by a certain kind of masculine sentiment. A "mail call" scene encourages stories of wives, moms, and girlfriends back home, of what the soldier is missing among friends and family, of homesickness. Usually, a raw recruit evokes sympathy because the hardened vets at first resist getting to know him (just more cannon fodder no one has the energy to mourn), but his earnest patriotism and courage win them over. The unit is led by a tough but fair (and, on occasion, sympathetic) father-figure sergeant. The men mourn their comrades killed in senseless violence by implacable enemies. The death of a beloved brother soldier might get a somber nighttime funeral with a plainspoken but moving eulogy. The unit probably has one member distrusted by most of his squad but is redeemed by the film's end with a sacrificial act that saves one or more comrades. The classic combat movie, concentrating on a squad representing America's ethnic diversity, ultimately reaffirms the American mission of civic equality, integrity, and the rewards of character and hard work over inherited privilege.[96]

Jimmy's war comics suggest none of these sentimental convictions. His troops exhibit no ethnic diversity. While they talk tough American slang, there are no scenes of complaining about the typical targets of military life: the food, boredom, bad officers, or chickenshit details. No selfish or cowardly soldiers are redeemed by heroism in the end. While the stories are marked by courageous actions and heroic deaths, their abiding tone is grim determination, commitment to vengeance, and the annihilation of the enemy without remorse.

The most cinematic, dynamic and, at times, lurid aspects of combat found their way into Jimmy's comics. Walter Wanger's *Gung Ho!* (1943) depicted Colonel Carlson's Makin Island Raiders, Marines who express racist judgments about the Japanese and who kill with conviction, from stabbing to shooting to strangulation. The film's Japanese have no honor, willing to descend to any ruse or betrayal. In Jimmy's comics, besides the vicious machine-gunning of defenseless parachuted pilots, Toads murder captured Frog POWs (as depicted in Lewis Milestone's 1944 *The Purple Heart*) and attack civilians with impunity (as with the portrait of Japanese artillery directed against an orphanage in *Bataan* and Robert Florey's 1945 *God is My Co-Pilot*). Toad bombers target clearly marked hospitals and Red Cross stations (as in *The Battle of Midway*). In Jimmy's war, bombing is precise and indiscriminate; the Toads target civilians and kill them with a technical efficiency possible only in movies and comics. The reality of "precision bombing" was quite different.[97] Since there are no women in any of Jimmy's combat panels, he depicted none of the assaults, rapes, and murders emphasized in *Behind the Rising Sun* and Ray Enright's 1945 *China Sky* or implied in a range of wartime comic books.

But Jimmy added a scene that would not have survived wartime censors. In "The Battle of Toadajima," Frogs pour flamethrowers into a Toad pillbox. A Toad engulfed in flames runs screaming from his hiding place, collapsing in a burning pile. Similar images, though sanitized, came early in war films such as *Guadalcanal Diary* (Lewis Seiler, 1943).[98] After the press reported on the Japanese torture of American POWs in early 1944, the OWI permitted the film industry to put such scenes in their movies. By 1945, newsreel footage of combat exposed far more of the war's brutality. Newsreel coverage of combat was visceral, its "you are there" images powerfully emotive in driving narratives that seemed so much more gripping and "realistic" than printed accounts in newspapers.[99] By the end of the war, the American public saw atrocity footage of the European camps and extermination.[100] But even the most explicit documentaries of island combat, such as *With the Marines at Tarawa* (1944) and *Fury in the Pacific* (1945)—which today remain difficult to watch—stopped at showing only the aftermath of the burned bodies.[101]

Scenes of massed soldiers, in beach landings and assaults on pillboxes, would have been time-consuming to draw. Jimmy was satisfied with distilling war to its most basic elements. Hand-to-hand combat in these panels moves in a staccato fashion. Any intervening movements between blows or kicks were ignored. Jimmy illustrated only the blows delivered. In a few cases, a threatening action by one opponent delivers the momentary anticipation of a violent response. The result is a breathless pace in ceaseless motion. These duels seem to reach a pitch with depictions of a flurry of blows, characterized by multiple motion lines, clouds of dust suggesting the force from landed fists, and stars declaring sharp pain.

Jimmy's fight scenes are as reminiscent of depictions of fighting in V. T. Hamlin's *Alley Oop* as perhaps any other comic. Hamlin's depictions of fights involving the short-tempered, club-swinging caveman illustrated heavy punches provoking several pain stars. The illustrators of *Batman* and *Captain America* at that time occasionally used stars but more often surrounded the fist's blow with something like a small burst. Stars surrounding the blow, especially multiple ones, suggested a slapstick quality about fighting avoided by the more "serious" superhero comics. Yet like the superhero comic, Jimmy wanted to resolve comic conflict with punching.[102] A certain kind of cinematic drama can increase the tension of a gunfight; in a sense, it must. The gun is quick, often decisive. If depicting that fight requires seeing the struggle's moment-by-moment dance, the artist needs close-ups of characters slowly walking to their fate, of tense bodies, of unblinking eyes and hard-set faces. But Jimmy's combatants knock guns from hands or dive into the arms of gun-wielding foes. This leveled the battleground to fists, kicks, and the rest of the ritual of hand-to-hand combat.

Jimmy's quick pacing of the fights, with little or no maneuvering but spiced with lots of clever banter, was right in line with the comic masters (figs. 1.14 and 1.15). Jimmy combined punching with kicks and knees to the stomach and always included one episode of grappling with the opponent's wrists. These brawls had no rules; anything goes to kill an antagonist. The fight scenes are no more cinematically complex than any other panel; Jimmy preferred to arrange scenes in the same flattened profile manner. Even if he set his fights in apparently dense jungles, he concentrated on clearing space for the battling Toad and Frog uninterrupted by branches, vines, or dangerous animals. The quick-witted, grimly humored exchanges between them seem to be common qualities of comic combatants.

These fights end with dramatic, vicious flair: throat-slitting, stabbing, or strangulation. This kind of mayhem runs throughout the entire body of Jimmy's work. While some fights conclude with a

Figure 1.14 V. T. Hamlin, *Alley Oop*, Saturday, March 11, 1939.

Figure 1.15 From *Batman* #1 (1940).

shooting, even these, typically, are at close quarters. Like Fletcher Hanks's *Stardust* and the villainous criminals of Chester Gould's *Dick Tracy*, strangulation seems among the most striking and personal depictions of assault. Stardust's omnipotent, crushing grip on the wicked reduces them to wads of flesh. Mrs. Pruneface slowly strangles and drowns a young man in a pool, a cruel fate Gould draws out by interspersing the murder frame by frame with scenes of concerned people searching for the victim.[103] Jimmy's combatants also revel in their grim work (pages 134–35). His preferred depictions of fighting were intimate. Face-to-face, rivals could exchange their black-humored insults. His Frogs, as well as his Toads, were unimpeded by second thoughts, by concerns of mercy or compassion. Only a couple of times do the combatants take POWs. Even then, the momentary truce immediately breaks down, and vicious hand-to-hand fighting erupts again. The soldiers of the opposing armies are strangers to one another. Their only expression of intimacy is their commitment to kill their rivals in the closest possible quarters.[104]

Jimmy dramatized war as a series of duels. He followed the same model when re-creating aerial combat derived from movies and comics. Before the war with Japan, airplanes and airpower were a rapidly growing staple of American popular culture. Their modernity, speed, and visual energy seemed revolutionary. Early movies like 1942's *Air Force* and many that followed depicted an American military airpower promising a decisive, rapid response against treachery and tyranny. The same year, the book *Victory Through Air Power* by the former Russian combat pilot and American aeronautics businessman Alexander P. de Seversky sold well and was disseminated further in a variety of middlebrow venues. The book so impressed Walt Disney that in 1943 he released an animated feature based on it; the film appeared in Lexington in early December 1943.[105]

How might this film have encouraged Jimmy's cartoons? The second half of *Victory Through Air Power* moves rapidly. The typically silhouetted ships and planes always deliver accurate blows to enemy forces. On occasion, the artists depict the Japanese with racist stereotypes. The animation suggests how modern aerial attack has made the world so much smaller. Its account of futuristic, industrialized, and scientifically advanced weapons drives home the vulnerability of the US against Germany's industrial might and Japan's air control of the Pacific, highlighting thousands of planes and thousands of tanks and submarines. German and Japanese factories turn out uncounted weapons, a kind of *Metropolis* of warfare. But in response, America's future planes will be scientific wonders of size, power, accuracy, and killing power. Finally, the film defends the "strategic" bombing of industry and dams; it even imagines new "gigantic bombs" to provoke destructive earthquakes. As Seversky argues, this kind of offense is the best defense. There is no sense that each side will face the other with equally deadly weapons in a future arms race. This film defends "total war" and civilian bombing; it even glories in it. Jimmy's portraits of the Toads' strategic bombing not only re-creates atrocity stories in wartime movies and comics but may also suggest how he interpreted reports of Allied and Axis use of air power against civilian centers.[106]

Jimmy's air power frames move at the same rapid pace as his depictions of hand-to-hand battles, from fighters maneuvering against their enemy to close-ups of pilots talking in clever, darkly humored exchanges. Still, far more of the aerial combat scenes have no dialogue at all. He got right to the point: the dynamics of planes hurtling through the sky toward other planes, aircraft carriers, or troops on the ground. The ratio of depicting tanks, ships, or artillery to their explosions implies swift destruction. It is hard not to think that every plane, ship, and artillery carefully drawn by Jimmy is also lovingly rendered as thrilling flame bursts and debris. Whether these kinds of attacks fall on Frogtown, another place like Lexington but one that was destroyed, or the jungle, Jimmy enjoyed imagining mayhem. His air war followed the dramatic and spectacular mythologies of technical wizardry and precision portrayed in war movies and comics.

The treacherous Toads clearly stood for the Japanese. Or did they? Jimmy modeled the Toad helmets on the German *Stahlhelm*. In "The Battle of Toadajima," an exchange between two Toad soldiers in the jungle has one call out, "Hans?" Beyond their distinctive appearances, the Toads and Frogs—like Homer's Trojans and Achaeans—seem to speak the same language. A more likely model was Hamlin's time-traveling couple, Alley Oop and Ooola, who could understand and be understood by anyone, anywhere, in the past or future.[107] The Frog and Toad industrial military seem to parallel one another, and their weapons appear identical. The Toad navy appears to have more aircraft carriers, while the Frogs have island air bases for launching attacks. While the ocean war and jungle settings suggest that Jimmy channeled typical images of "Asiatic" cruelty and savage deception, he clearly built his confrontation as he wished. As the son of proud German immigrants, many of whom still spoke German at home, Jimmy may have been both self-conscious of and sensitive to his own ethnic identity. But this is impossible to know.[108]

Jimmy seemed happy to reproduce many of the stereotyped, bigoted, even racist elements of the worst of American propaganda and exaggeration. His father belonged to the KKK. What effect did that have on him? Racism's stereotyped, universal, and undifferentiated portraits of an entire people, where the simplified individual stands in for the group, emphasizes their despicable moral character. Their opponent has the license to destroy such enemies. But in the war stories, the Frogs quickly prove themselves as suited to vicious combat and merciless vengeance as the Toads. Elsewhere, Jimmy drew evil Frogs and later winged Frogs in the same manner as the Toads. The characterization of the eyes and teeth, their cruelty and viciousness, marked malevolence—but not necessarily distinctions of a racial nature. Neither character bears any particular skin color other than the Frog's spots.[109] Yet the Toads' relentless cruelty reflects American propaganda suggesting that Japanese soldiers were the contrasting image of the American male soldier: cunning, determined contrivances of warfare.[110] Toad behavior generally echoed common media portraits of the Japanese.

Why Frogs?

According to a former classmate, Jimmy and Jack Kutz invented the "Frogs," constantly drawing them in and out of class (fig. 1.16).[111] The classmate recalled that Kutz and Kugler were inseparable; they spoke in a language they invented and created silly walks and odd gestures they paraded for their classmates throughout the school halls.[112] Another classmate recalled that Kutz was also an accomplished artist.[113] Throughout those school years, the *Clipper* reported that Jimmy and other classmates often displayed their art in class, whether on the blackboard during the holidays or posted elsewhere in the classroom.[114] The seventh-grade art teacher at the West Ward school may have encouraged this work since cartooning was part of the curriculum. That was not unusual in American schools.[115] This, and the classmate's recollection that Jimmy and his friend Jack were drawing frogs in the eighth grade (possibly even the seventh), would date the comics to 1944 and 1945. But another classmate recalled that Jimmy and Kutz passed Frog cartoons around among students at Lexington High School in the years 1946–1950. Since he titled one chapter "Toadajima," Jimmy almost certainly drew the comics after the war.[116]

Figure 1.16

While it is impossible to say with certainty when he first drew them, reports of the conflict, films, and comic books would have given him all the inspiration he needed.

But still, "Frogs"? What follows is speculation built on memories of conversations with my father, some surviving books he owned, and examples from contemporary comic art of that world. My father often described how he spent a good deal of his childhood hunting, not only with a rifle but as an amateur naturalist. He claimed that an abandoned greenhouse sat behind one of his homes where he kept the wolf spiders, mice, bats, salamanders, rattlesnakes, and other animals he caught. He may have begun that hobby quite early; later, he also kept scrapbooks with pictures of birds and other animals.[117] Just before or while in high school, Jimmy acquired two large hardbound books, Sherman C. Bishop's *Handbook of Salamanders* (1943) and Raymond Ditmars's *Reptiles of North America* (1907, 1942). These standard and oft-reprinted scientific handbooks, guides to his interest in Lexington-area wildlife, may have also encouraged his cartooning choice of Frogs.[118] Of course, "funny animal" cartoons are an old tradition. How-to cartooning manuals of the period suggested animal characters were a good place for children to learn to draw. Those cartoon frogs are instantly recognizable: squat, round amphibians with large eyes and great, wide mouths. They are humorous, and their exaggerated postures and accessories recall river life, with a banjo or guitar and a jug of some tasty drink set in the lazy days of summer.[119]

But Jimmy's characters are not typical of any frog-like comic character. Thin and angular, his Frogs stand upright. In fact, they are minimally animal-like. With few exceptions, they have no tails but often have a single dark spot on their backs. They have the faintest hint of webbed feet but no webbed hands. Most distinctive are their long, narrow faces with a clear overbite. Only their oversized, rounded eyes seem typical of cartoon animals.[120] Toads particularly, but also evil or cruel Frogs, had narrowed eyes and sharp teeth. Occasionally, these Frogs are larger, darker, or hairier (fig. 1.17, in a pose similar to that of the Japanese soldier in the ad for *Behind the Rising Sun*, in fig. 1.7). This panel, one of Jimmy's experiments or unfinished brief stories, captures the Frog's simplicity while suggesting how a few carefully chosen additions could develop it into the character's evil shadow. Wartime and combat comics often turned to animal portraits of combatants: the Nazis and Japanese were often rats, skunks, or monkeys. Hitler could appear as a pig, an octopus, or a spider; or Goebbels as a rodent.[121] Jimmy's Frogs did not capture some basically inhuman or contemptuous quality. They are largely cartoon people with animal faces.[122]

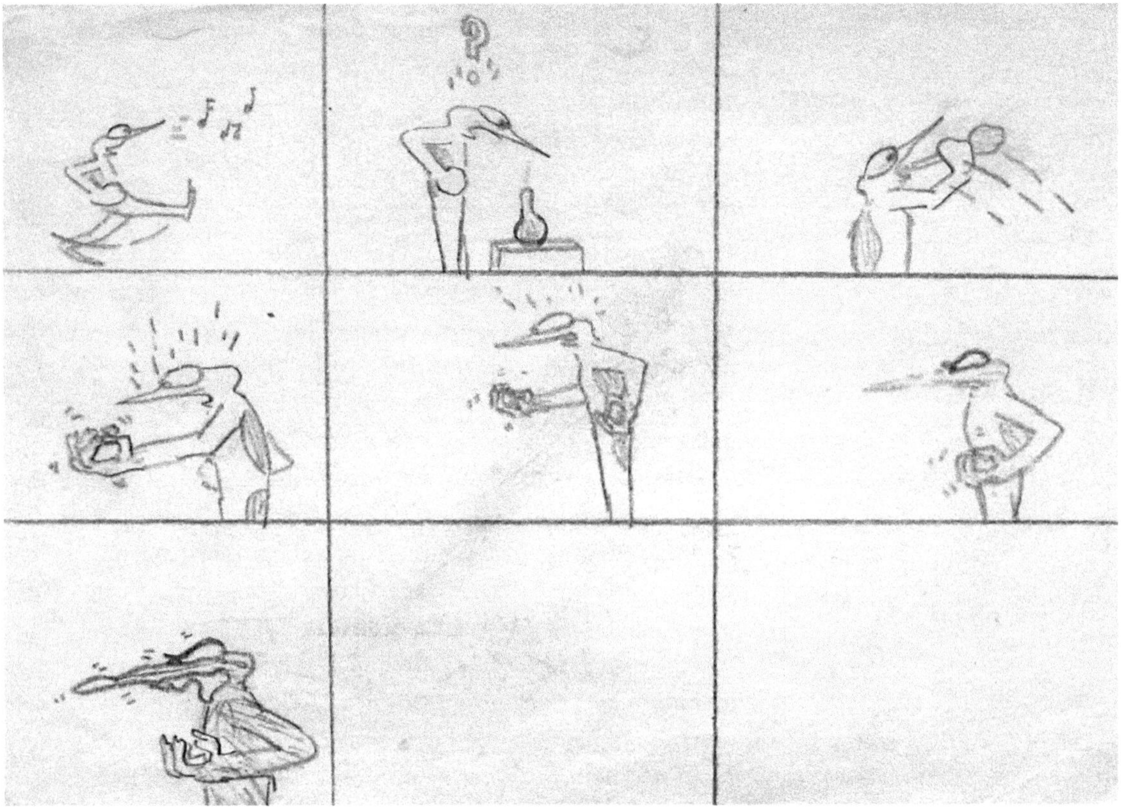

Figure 1.17

Yet, strangely, Frog soldiers don't seem to wear clothing. Their pilots have fur-lined gear; the Frog spy at the start of "The Fate of a Toad Convoy" wears a shirt and slacks. But the soldiers are barefoot, their dark spot apparent on their backs, wearing only ammo belts and helmets. Toads are fully uniformed, including jackboots. Can amphibious creatures perhaps go naked while land creatures must wear clothing? Perhaps Jimmy had no other reason for these artistic choices than to keep the Frog/Toad distinction clear. But there

Figure 1.18 Gus Edson, *The Gumps*, December 8, 1952.

is, perhaps, an underlying logic to these choices, including even the possible innocence of Frogs who have no need for clothing, let alone the uniforms of the mechanized, "jackbooted" Toads.

The stocky, plump frog is more immediately laughable, inviting the reader into a truly fantastic world of the strange physical laws of slapstick drama.[123] Jimmy's comics are far more "realistic," aspiring to imitation, though idealized and amplified in their own ways of the world at war. He did make some effort to draw detailed planes, tanks, and other weaponry. While his Frogs are iconic cartoon figures, they are not immediately *comic* or humorous figures. That would likely distract from their flying fighter bombers, throwing hand grenades, or bayoneting the enemy. Their humor is the grim irony of life-or-death struggles. Further, their sharply angular joints, emphasized in movement, augment their fundamental status as dynamic. Jimmy drew his Frogs as if they rarely rest. They stroll; they hustle; when they fight, it is all levers driving blow upon blow upon blow on an opponent. Even merely talking, their long, narrow beaks imply a sharp challenge.

Characters with extreme overbites were not unusual; among the best-known were Sidney Smith's popular syndicated strip *The Gumps* (1917–1959). By the 1930s, *The Gumps* had made it to animated film

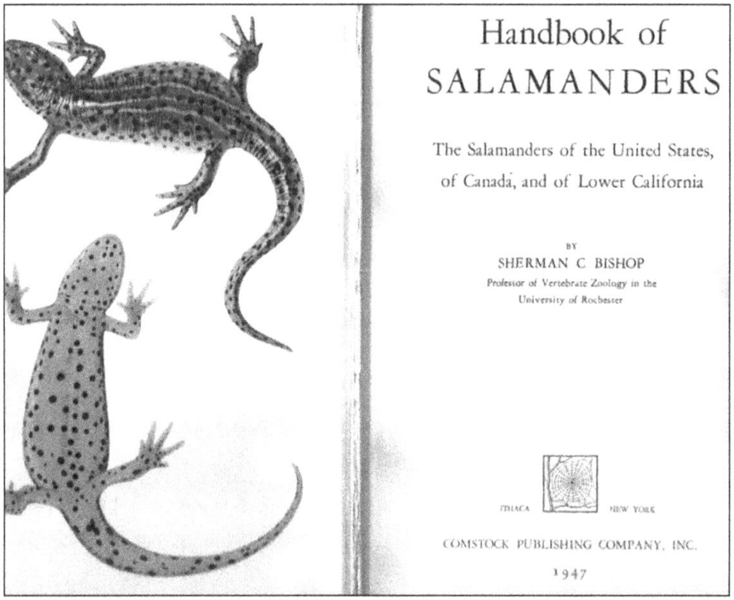
Handbook of
SALAMANDERS

The Salamanders of the United States,
of Canada, and of Lower California

BY
SHERMAN C. BISHOP
Professor of Vertebrate Zoology in the
University of Rochester

ITHACA NEW YORK

COMSTOCK PUBLISHING COMPANY, INC.

1947

Figure 1.19

Figure 1.20 Ub Iwerks, "Flip the Frog," from *Fiddlesticks* (1930).

and radio as well as toys (fig. 1.18).[124] Further, Jimmy's Frogs, thin and angular, resemble in some way the salamanders of Bishop's illustrations (fig. 1.19). Other qualities recall certain characters from animated shorts, including Ub Iwerks's Disney figures like Mickey Mouse of the 1930s and 1940s.[125] Iwerks also designed "Flip the Frog" shorts of the 1930s. Flip's stocky, neckless body, broad mouth and big, round eyes were typical for an animated frog. But some characteristics resemble those of Jimmy's Frogs: long, thin arms and legs, upright walk, and sharply webbed feet (fig. 1.20).[126]

Jimmy's Frogs, though distinctive and inventive, are deceptively uncomplicated. We see them side-on, echoing the earliest cave paintings and Ancient Near Eastern relief carvings, similar to his ships, tanks, and planes. Drawing characters in profile saves time and energy.

Getting the essential details right through repetition meant refining his craft as he had distilled it down to just what he wanted. Distillation prevented the temptation for baroque clutter. While naïve, such a style was important for accomplishing his goals; those goals seemed to be moving onto and through the action. Jimmy's comics are always on the move to collisions of metal, bodies, bullets, and fists. Exposition sets the circumstances for those collisions, with only the barest of written narrative. The expository scenes restrain, just barely, the artist's building anticipation of the nearly anarchic frenzy of combat. The Frog is a distinctive, serviceable humanoid for the war stories, even funny looking, and with a handful of deft strokes, easily transformed into a vicious, merciless fighter.

Why were Jimmy's war comic characters not more human appearing? The Frogs give him some emotional distance, a permission to distill war to its most violent and cruel confrontations but without the effect of dehumanizing cruelty. The strange Frog character makes Jimmy's war just alien enough to permit settling into that world according to the logic of its own peculiar drama. The Frog's strangeness encourages a smirking kind of laughter, more in the company of the black humor of his morally thin comic universe. The Frogs mark Jimmy's entrance, and ours, into his mayhem-laden fantasy of the real world. Perhaps the best response to the Frog character is: well, *why not?*

Conclusion

On Christmas Day, 1941, the *Dawson County Herald* offered the headline "Cozad Young Man Dies After Having to Cut Off His Own Left Arm." Twisted inside a corn picker, he amputated the arm with his pocketknife and then drove eight miles to the doctor before dying. It seems odd on the holiday to report mayhem in such surprising detail.

But people are curious about such awfulness, so out of the ordinary, so shocking and sudden. Against this background of occasional violence, Jimmy's adolescent curiosity reached the height of inspiration through the reporting of combat in Europe and the Pacific. Jimmy imitated the comic conventions best suited to tell and "see" what he imagined: explosions, aerial dogfights, gun fighting, fist fights, sword fights, strangulations, and maiming. He unleashed his comic strip imagination onto a bare structure of the coverage of the war. In this context, Jimmy's comic strip violence and anarchistic dark humor are not surprising. The literary historian and veteran military pilot Samuel Hynes argued that war creates strange, even peculiar, kinds of violence, maiming, and death, later shaped poetically into memoirs creating what he called the "battlefield gothic."[127] In the comic strips first inspired by the war, Jimmy tried to create images conjuring some part of the bizarre, fascinating, and awful spectacle of mass violence.

Jimmy had reached into the swirling waters of national wartime radio, film, and comics running through Lexington and pulled out . . . violent stories. I've tried reaching into the debris of his world to tell a different kind of story. The comics were Jimmy's joyful re-creation of an adult culture he translated into his imagined pencil forms. The war was not merely the production of an entertainment industry of film, radio, and comic books. It had true combat, real enemies, palpable fear, expressions of meaning and purpose, and loss and despair. Yet, World War II was ideally suited, by its character and era, for dramatization. Perhaps most war stories are for a civilian audience, eager to reaffirm national glory, excitement, brave adventure, and somber reflections on noble sacrifice. The US press that reported combat were largely extensions of the military themselves, obeying image-conscious—if not obsessed—leaders eager to win the war of public opinion at home. War machines speeding through the sky, at sea, and on earth were the perfect subjects for film and radio. Before TV, radio broadcasts invited listeners to imagine with almost unrivaled vividness the immediacy of combat. All this was translated, for millions of children and adolescents, into comic strip and comic book forms.[128]

In Jimmy's war, his combatants enthusiastically jump into a thrilling life of adventure seemingly far from the calm dependability and predictability of small-town life. They are not superheroes in any typical sense. His comics have genre elements associated with popular war stories, beginning with a mission, a military objective. Exposition and icons of military planning, such as maps, orient the reader. The drama begins with an aerial invasion, provoking a fighting response. The nearly subhuman enemy requires equal brutality. Depictions of combat are often reduced to a duel between two implacable foes, and the story often concludes with a climactic battle involving all the combatants. Since he did not complete the "Famous War," we do not know where he would have taken the story. There is no decisive victory, no final surrender, no armistice. No leaders commit suicide rather than submit, leaving their remaining soldiers and civilians to a cataclysmic end. There are no concentration camps or unforgettable hills of human corpses waiting for mass graves. There is no final, ruthless invasion of the defeated opposing capital, no formal surrender of forces on the deck of the victor's battleship following an apocalyptic bombing of two cities. There is little in the "Famous War" to suggest Jimmy was interested in such matters of a war's end. As far as we can tell, the Frogs and Toads just keep fighting, through the staccato rhythms of small, square frames.

Jimmy's war, consistent with the classic combat movie (but unlike the generic Western), features no women.[129] Since there is nothing superhero-like about his characters, it is not surprising that Jimmy gave them none of the hypermasculine muscularity of Superman or

Captain America. Consistent with the funny animal style, there is nothing muscular at all about the Frogs and Toads. The skinny characters contrast their undefined physiques against their frantic dynamism of movement, especially in a fight. It is perhaps no coincidence that his male-only enterprise lacks the sentimental, humanizing elements of the typical combat genre. Yet that dynamism was necessary to the masculine depiction of combat, typical of commercial wartime comics and war movies. As US propaganda repeated, war was a mostly male enterprise. Jimmy's combatants suggest masculinity, not in an artistic ideal of the perfect male body but in their psychology and actions: their vengeance-fueled determinism, their grim commitment to fighting and annihilating the enemy.[130] In a sense, Jimmy's masculine cartoon world displays its greatest contrast, in the superhero genre, against Wonder Woman. William Moulton Marston's unusual (for the times) feminist convictions gave eager readers after 1942 a challenger to the typical superhero male punch-ups. He believed the character was ideally suited to the moral training of American youth during World War II. Wonder Woman would teach women's virtues and powers, in particular, the wisdom of a loving submission to kind, wise authority.[131] If there is any such earnestness in Jimmy's comics, it is in their violent though peculiarly masculine dynamism.

Jimmy did not soften or domesticate his typically lone but violent characters by reference to mothers, girlfriends, or children back home. He was apparently uninterested in providing reassurance that, once the war ended, the soldier would rediscover his humanity, a reassurance signified in movie and comic book by narrated memories of home, women, and family. Jimmy's characters express little or no sentiments other than a desire for vengeance, grim courage, and cutting humor. There's no talk of each soldier surrendering his own needs or convictions to "the team." His comics are fantasies of struggle and adventure beyond Lexington, but also beyond ideal moral bounds. I hesitate to read his depictions of guns, knives, swords, and cunning to reflect much of anything about small-town America. Bearing arms, hunting, and occasional struggles against the authorities are typical parts of American life. The overriding sense that "nothing ever happens" or "there is nothing to do" could encourage rebellion; the relationships of small-town citizens with the different authorities made anonymity difficult. The anarchic tone of the comics could be consistent with one young man's possible response to progressive educational pedagogy, to small-town authority, and during the war, to the authorized violence of the state. He may well have seen the modern school as defining "normal" with which he used his comics to pick a fight.

As historian Steven Mintz has argued, the cultures created and overseen by children and adolescents are marked by fantasy as well as struggles with adults for independence and autonomy.[132] It is possible Jimmy's vengeful, violent stories drew fuel from the struggles he witnessed during the Depression, his parents' failed marriage, or his difficult home life. But the appeal of propaganda, movies, and comic books alongside adventure, often violent, is not hard to understand in the most positive circumstances. Yet that appeal perhaps increased in an era marked by confusion, regret, loneliness, or loss. When psychiatrist Dr. Lauretta Bender testified before the House Subcommittee on Juvenile Delinquency (Comic Books) in 1954 (the hearings made famous partly for the testimony of comic book enemy Fredric Wertham), she recalled her little boy's affection for comic book depictions of violence:

> My second son, who was a little older and a different type of child, instead of rejecting it has tried to solve the problem [of suffering and death] . . . he loves to watch for hours on end television, radio, and movies which deal with these subjects.

> I think for him it is an effort to find a solution of the mystery of life and death and how it can happen that a child's father can leave him even before the child knows the father.[133]

It is tempting to speculate on Jimmy's home life inspiring his comic violence. But what is more certain, as well as interesting, is how small-town Nebraska seemed as capable of provoking his strange, obsessive, and disturbing comic strip stories as the urban East Coast cities we associate with the great comic artists, often the children of Jewish immigrants.[134] Small-town midwestern kids like Jimmy are harder to find reflected in typical histories of American youth, certainly as the inventors of the comic book.[135] In retrospect, he anticipated, indirectly in the war comics but more so in later stories, themes of William Gaines's horror and crime tales in the EC comics of the early 1950s.[136] Further—and perhaps deeper, because school was the primary authoritative institution in his life—Jimmy's comics seem a direct affront to the goals of educational reformers of that era, working hard to regulate the minds and bodies of their students. During the war, the media depicted the close cooperation of government and popular culture to present a unified war effort to the public. This can be seen, for example, in a full-page ad promoting the local Lexington schools for "the Progressive Education of Young Americans."[137] If his eighth-grade teacher suggested that Jimmy's hygiene required "urgent attention," it was perhaps from too much time sweating over Frogs and Toads.[138]

Progressive educational reform and national propaganda about the war reached deeply into rural America, and Jimmy did not have to live in a cultural center or big city to see it for himself and to talk back to it in his own way. But consider the great Marvel Comics artist Steve Ditko, who left behind little to manifest the inner landscape of his youth, certainly not of his adolescent art. Comics scholar Blake Bell hesitated to speculate on the scant evidence available about Ditko's youthful influences, though reaching similar conclusions as I have suggested about Jimmy's comics and intentions: "With Ditko's early personal history being somewhat of a 'locked drum,' it's difficult to ascertain where the seeds may have been planted that would see him craft such flamboyant scenes of decapitation, acid baths, and eye gouging. There is little evidence in his youth of anything but an ordinary, small-town American life in the Depression and WWII years." Ditko's early work in horror apparently developed from his obsessive craftsmanship as well as his ambition to do whatever it took to make it as a comic artist.[139] Jimmy was not nearly Ditko's equal as a draftsman. He did not turn his adolescent obsession into professional ambition. But his work was hardly less devoted or audacious.

The war stories required traveling beyond the safe and familiar to the unpredictable and threatening. Jimmy's imagination moved into the excitement and power of creating, sustaining, and drafting images of challenge and even terror. Horror, after all—intentionally depicting monstrous evil, satisfying a fascination with it in order to provoke dread, basic disgust, or shock—typically occurs in everyday affairs.[140] Setting key parts of his war story in an imagined Lexington encouraged a thrill from war's mayhem right at home. Doing so, he may have gained a sense of membership and purpose in sharp contrast to an adult world in which he could not have enjoyed much real authority.[141] Jimmy's comic strip world, in one sense, expresses how successfully the various agencies of the federal government, local news media, and popular culture mediums cooperated to offer a nearly seamless portrait of warfare and their national enemies. This represented the "mythmaking" of "the best war ever," as Michael Adams described it.[142] But Jimmy's myth distilled away much of the patriotic chest-pounding of the popular portrayals of the war. He could revel in versions of the battlefield grotesque without any of the shock, horror, or despair of combat's nightmarish character. For example, one study of the war's combat casualties concluded that about eighty-five percent came from shells, bombs, and grenades, and less than ten percent from bullets.[143] Action movies and adventure comic books depend on the far more dramatic combat confrontation of individuals shooting at each other. Building his own world from those images, Jimmy took creative control of the events of massive, modern, and dynamic machine warfare, capable of destruction both terrifying and exciting. He joined the world of cartoonists and storytellers, where he had the power to manipulate images to what he wanted to see.[144] Jimmy's cartoon violence contributed to the violation, at least temporarily, of the adult world of moralism, a stance typical of comics and comic strips in the late 1930s and early 1940s.[145]

These war stories starkly contrasted with the life-affirming themes in wartime advertising and government propaganda. As Robert Westbrook has argued, defending the family was central to corporate ads supporting the war in the "Why We Fight" tenor. Many of these ads described a united America while highlighting the protection of values favoring a liberal, individualistic society, including those of personal prosperity. They depicted servicemen and servicewomen, as well as civilians, gladly sacrificing to protect their own families and fellow citizens back home.[146] Jimmy's comics are, unsurprisingly, much more naïve. Frog soldiers do not talk about home and their families, fighting to protect them from another Toad invasion. They rarely talk about home at all. They live, like their Toad opponents, entirely in the moment of combat, recalling the deadly earlier fights, engaging wave upon wave of Toad forces, and, if they survive, steeling themselves for the next assault. Since the war began with a sneak attack, the Frogs fight because their foe is merciless and implacable; the Toads fight with relentless cruelty which further inspires the Frogs' desire for vengeance. But as I said, the Frogs do not reminisce about home, memories of laughter at holidays, and delicious home-cooked meals or their high school sweethearts. As equally determined and vicious as the Toads, the Frogs express no more virtue or commitment to the liberal values of democracy, the famous "Four Freedoms" of Norman Rockwell's wartime paintings, than the Toads themselves.

Not merely anarchic, there is something futuristic about Jimmy's love of accelerated motion, collision, explosion, and complex fighting with war machines, rifles, pistols, and explosives. He moved the action into the jungle, not just once, but twice. Why? Because the jungle was not Lexington. The jungle was utterly unlike the Midwest Plains: ancient, labyrinthine, and darkly deadly, a rich, iconic landscape so unlike Nebraska and yet probably just as confusing, at times lonely and even frightening in its own way.[147] In horror-movie style, the innocent snap of a branch exposes the soldier, releasing hell (see p. 131). Yet Jimmy ignored most of the genre's key elements, much of which began in the late 1920s with Hal Foster's daily and Rex Maxon's Sunday *Tarzan*, and Alex Raymond and Don Moore's 1934's *Jungle Jim*. Tarzan did not earn his own comic book until Dell Comics launched him in 1947, drawn by Jesse Marsh, Russ Manning, and Doug Wildey. A decade sooner, Sheena, Queen of the Jungle, debuted in Fiction House's *Jumbo Comics*; in 1940, they started *Jungle Comics* with Kaanga, Lord of the Jungle. Even so, jungle adventures did not really clear a path until after the war. With all this potential inspiration at his disposal, Jimmy's jungle had no dangerous animals, exhausting heat, or drenching rain.[148] Nor did he need the staples of American depictions of Africa in jungle comic books: wide-eyed natives speaking pidgin, ruled by benevolent colonists and missionary medics, threatened by their evil counterparts or local shamans.[149]

As was his narrative style, he distilled the jungle setting to the bare essentials, counting on the reader to bring his past reading and viewing experience to complete the silent dread of such a foreign place.

In redrafting much of a world war's adventures onto Lexington's scale, Jimmy turned the local into something strange, even eerie. Though he set most of his war stories in faraway ocean battlefields and jungles, the settings for the Toad invasion represent the neighborhoods, homes, and buildings familiar to him. If Jimmy read *Dick Tracy* and other comics and saw a range of films, he had plenty of cityscapes to imitate. The haunts of *Superman* and *Batman* were the modernist vistas of Fritz Lang's *Metropolis* (1927); the superhero was born among those epic futurist Babels.[150] Jimmy could have chosen them for his fantasy war; his later comics have signs of them, especially in a *film noir* register. Yet the "Frogtown" attacked by the Toads has churches, homes, and libraries similar to the buildings of his childhood's Lexington, most still there today. What IF a nation of monstrous militarized killers attacked Lexington? What IF average small-town citizens marshaled their industry and wits to take the war to their Toad enemies?[151] The gleeful anarchy of Jimmy's futuristic combat was just as meaningful to a Waspy Nebraskan and just as at home in the reputedly reduced vistas of the Midwest as anywhere else.

Jimmy's war comics imagined combat violence as vicious as anything seen in films about the war through 1945. But his comic violence is possibly closer to the standard set by true-crime comics. Led by editor Charles Biro's inaugural *Crime Does Not Pay* in 1942, these pushed right against the borders of acceptable depictions of violence. Building on Hollywood's noir crime dramas of the late 1930s, these gory attempts at cautionary tales against criminal behavior, conflating violence with realism, attracted denunciation from educators and public intellectuals. Outraged reformers attempted housebreaking comic books years before Fredric Wertham's more famous crusades of the early 1950s.[152] Even the illustrators of such gothic comic book horror from Edgar Allan Poe's tales, like *The Black Cat*, limited their depictions of grisly murder to shadowed intimations of the act of murdering a woman with an ax, later portraying her corpse unharmed.[153] The fantastic exploits of superheroes in the war ran out of fuel even before 1945, but not the taste for brutal, adult-themed violence in comic form. Following closely along the dark avenue paced by crime comics, by the early 1950s, a new, grittier, and psychologically darker combat comic book, set in the Korean War, was marketed to adult males. The popularity of the combat film continued long after the fighting ceased, if anything encouraged by the war in Southeast Asia, and even more harsh in aspirations to combat realism.[154] Post-war tastes seemed primed for even more vivid transgressions of decency and taste.

If Jimmy began drawing his war comics near the end of the war or just after it, his imagined combat mayhem surely exceeded what was already being seen in most war films. Considering the cover art for many war comic books, in which beheadings, bayoneting, vivid bloodshed, and torture were typical, his was at least as violent.[155] His exhibition of cruel comedy mirrored the tone of Biro's *Crime Does Not Pay*, forecasting the macabre humor Gaines encouraged in EC's horror comics. Jimmy distilled popular and official portraits of combat, horror movies, and patriotically intended propaganda into his dynamic but morally thin retelling of the war.The fears of educators and psychologists of the inspiration of America's adolescent imaginations were apparently not groundless. Had educational reformers found comic strips like Jimmy's, it is not hard to imagine their diagnosis.

Historians of the comic book do not shy away from explaining the consequences of the war and popular cultural depictions of violence in Americans' preferences after 1945. For some, the war liberated the pent-up fantasies of masculinity and power exhibited in the superhero comics.[156] Post-war Americans, awash in the glow of victory, apparently struggled against the burden of world leadership, fear of atomic war with Russia, and the apparent moral collapse of the American ideal with new challenges to the family, juvenile delinquency, and divorce—all signs of a society in crisis.[157] The victory over one kind of totalitarianism appears to have given way to a cold war against another, with receding confidence that America could triumph again. The lurid violence and depraved cruelty of post-war crime and horror comics pointed to "masochistic expositions of American failures" and a "morbid fascination with depravity and self-destruction." True crime comics were therefore, according to these interpretations, a significant moment in the evolution of the comic book: from juvenile sentiments and relatively safe humor to unblinking depictions of American values and self-affirmation that are far, far darker.[158]

I am not confident there is evidence to assess something as broad and generalized as the post-1945 American psyche. It seems even less likely that we can read that mentality off of post-war comic books. While comic book sales for stories of the Cold War's atomic confrontation and espionage may tell us about such preoccupations, it is not clear that a taste for sensational, shocking stories and art tells us as much about our widespread anxiety, diminished confidence in the American Way, or fantasies of nihilism and immorality. Jimmy's comics, anticipating these ghastly shifts in taste, tell us, I believe, a good deal about what American youth could conceivably glean and repurpose from wartime mass media. But I am not convinced I can move from his comics to an assessment of his confidence for the future or his anxiety about post-war America. I think, instead, that the comics reflect his clever turning of what the adult authorities suggested was true, proper, and even virtuous about the war into something quite different. He intended them perhaps to provoke those authorities, exploiting the countercultural, anarchistic, even at times futuristically nihilistic rebellion of comics.

Chapter 1

What Started the War

A splash page introducing "the famous war" promises action in the air, on the ground, and below the surface. Evidence of erasing reveals that Jimmy considered "the famous *wars*" as a first title. His military insignia and flags for both forces suggest nothing American or Japanese. Both the Frog's dark, diagonal quarters and the Toad's contrasted horizontal lines might vaguely suggest the National Socialist *Balkenkreuz*, but that's not clear. The artistry here seems more accomplished than that of later stories. Did Jimmy possibly launch into the stories themselves, drawing the war's origins after he had told some of the combat tales, later completing the splash page? He could have drawn this last; perhaps he worked across months, even years. Again, there's no way to know any more than we know about the order of each chapter.

The war begins, but you see no Toads, just their fighters and bombers. You don't hear their radio chatter; nothing about the decision to invade. Not even a narrative ribbon. The silence heightens the enemy's mystery. The Toad attack erupts from the sky, beginning simply with "When. . . ." A cinematic POV from above captures the silhouetted planes. A single fighter turns its wings; *when*. . . .

The target, Frogtown, is on one of several Frog islands and has no apparent military presence, just a civilian harbor and airport. The Toads first bomb the church where most Frogs spend Sunday morning. Not too many years before, at age twelve, Jimmy had joined the local Presbyterian church, but his drawing does not imitate Lexington's Presbyterian sanctuary. A Toad fighter then cuts down a civilian. Fighter-bombers hit the responding firetruck; then a ship, then apartments and office buildings; they strafe women and children, a cruel scene possibly lifted from the opening of *Bataan* (1943). Finally, they attack the airport, manned only by WWI-era biplanes. The brief scenes of destruction depict utter devastation. Jimmy drew one corpse, but it was not cruelly maimed. The destruction is reminiscent of photos from the Pearl Harbor attack and other combat areas.

But this was not Pearl Harbor. Frogtown was entirely civilian, on the scale of Jimmy's hometown. Unlike the US preparation for a possible war with Japan and aid to Britain against Germany, the Frog military buildup comes only after the attack. Frogs rebuild their homes and community. They manufacture modern weapons like tanks, ships, fighter planes, and rifles. Interestingly, Jimmy included a knife and sword in the arsenal. His Frogs create an American-like military: Army, Navy, "Aircore," and Seabees. All wear uniforms except the Frog soldiers, who are clothed only in ammo belts and helmets. After completing the buildup and training, they make the "decoration of war." The Toads follow the attack on Frogtown by immediately attacking the other Frog islands.

Jimmy used a typical comic book convention of including hints of a larger world only glimpsed within the frame's limits (for example, dead Frogs lie outside the comic gutter). He would return to this later, depicting only a portion of a departing plane following its attack.

There are signs of his erasing and revising some of the narration, but none apparent in the images. This would hold true for the rest of the war comics. Jimmy may have revised the story's written narrative, but he seemed to have known precisely what he wanted to draw.

FROGS
TOADS
THE FAMOUS
WAR
OF THE FROGS AND TOADS

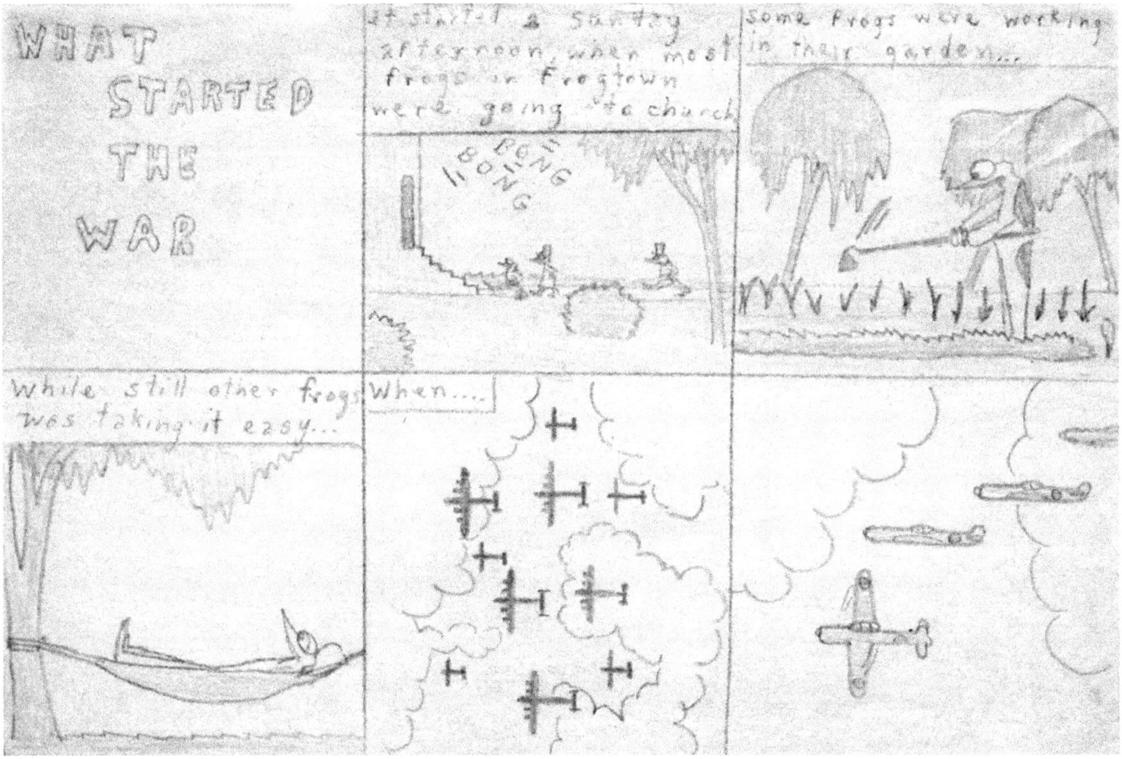
WHAT STARTED THE WAR
It started a Sunday
afternoon, when most
frogs in Frogtown
were going to church
BONG BONG
Some frogs were working
in their garden...
While still other frogs
was taking it easy...
When....

BONG
BONG
What goes on?
Ah-h-g-g!
E-E-E-E-E-E-E
F.D.

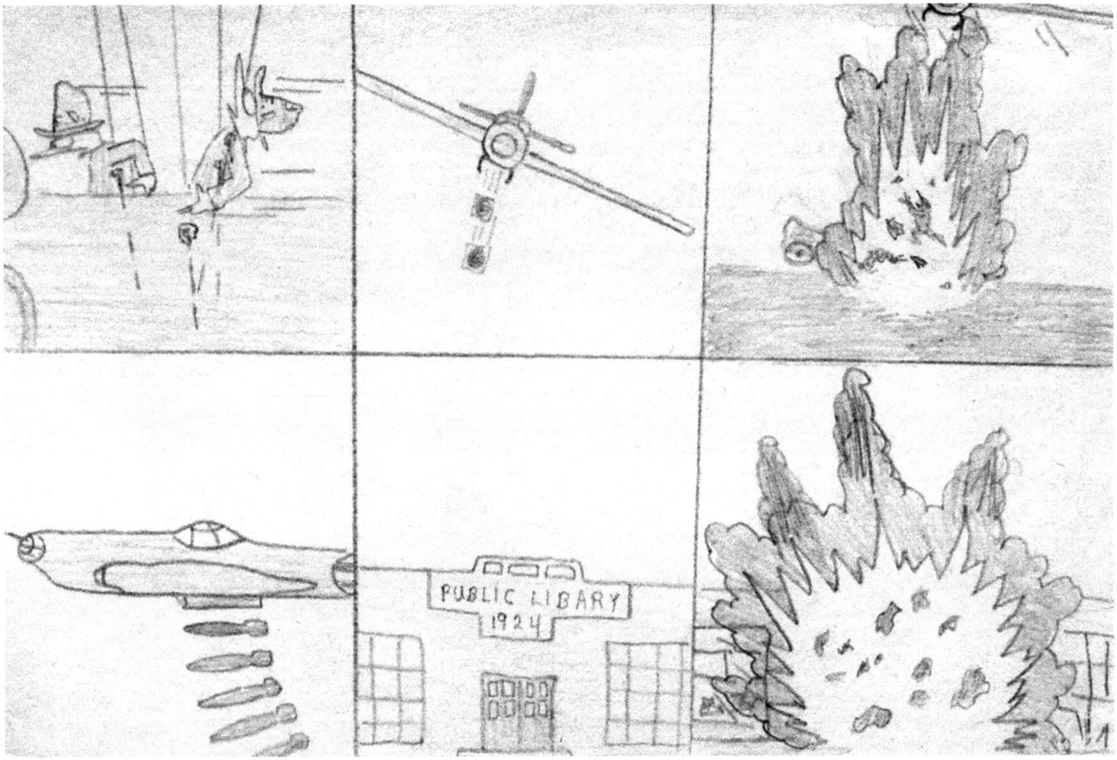
PUBLIC LIBARY
1924

Frog town's airportia

In a few short minutes the bombers complete their work, and head for home leaving the ruins of Frogtown!

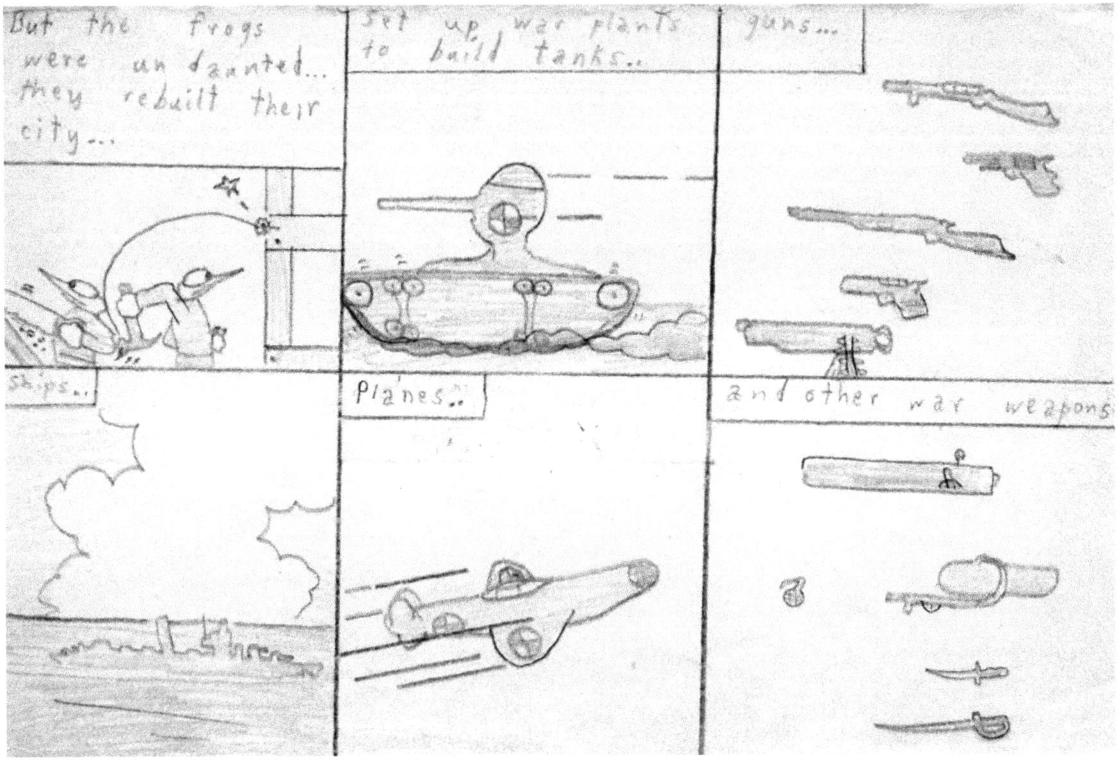
But the frogs were undaunted... they rebuilt their city...
set up war plants to build tanks..
guns...
ships..
planes..
and other war weapons

The frogs learned the art of self defence
learned the use of all weapons...
And of course started an...
Army
Navy
Aircore
Seabees
And as soon as these things were done, a decoration of war was started against the toads!!
The frogs did not have time to put men on all their islands before the toads landed, but those who were there met the toads in battle!

Chapter 2

The Fall of Frogington

For the first time since the opening splash page, we see the Toads. This chapter begins with another splash page, after which a Toad air attack promptly launches the action. Still struggling to recover from the initial assault, the Frogs have few defenses against a massed Toad force. This recalls the conditions of the American military in the Pacific early in the war, most famously the heroic but doomed defense of Wake Island hours after Pearl Harbor and several other battles throughout that theater.

The thrust of the hand to the starter; the first whirl of the prop; then the shimmering halo of a fighter about to ascend. In these few frames, Jimmy attempted a dramatic narrative. The plane's wheels retract on takeoff, lifting just as a Toad plane enters the scene and, in the sixth frame, a second Toad plane homes in on the Frog fighter. With the air war comes antiaircraft guns, and so the story moves back and forth from above to below. Burning fighters crash to the ground; crippled bombers fly directly toward the reader, then crash. Frog planes regularly receive fire, only to turn quickly and return it or, in a desperate final act of courage, drive their burning wrecks into midair collisions with the enemy, right out of contemporary war films and comic book covers.

But the airborne acrobatics give way to Toad paratroopers landing on Frogington. The battle spools out between outnumbered Frogs firing from pillboxes or laying dynamite traps. Again, Frogs die bravely, recklessly, to break the Toad attack, at least to take as many with them as possible. The genre's depictions of aerial fighting, of the wounded soldier falling over the TNT plunger as his last brave act, come right from mainstream cinema and combat comics. The dialogue is filled with slang conventions of comic and cinematic fighting: "What th—?," "Why you . . . !," etc. In Jimmy's war, machine guns lay down razor-sharp lines of deadly fire, cutting massed troops in multiple maiming. Explosions capture soldier and machine in a white-hot lightning strike of ruination. He had a practiced style for his explosions as well as the trajectory of bigger guns, with heat at the center of dense clouds, suspended on long shafts of propelled shells. His artillery details suggest early World War II types.

The sign of a Toad retreat prompts a cheer from the remaining Frog defenders. But the Toad forces merely needed to bring their "big guns" online against the town. As quickly as the invasion began, it ends with Frogington—by the map, about the size of Lexington—annihilated, summed up in the bombing of a block of apartments.

THE FALL
OF
FROGINGTON

Frogington has few defences becaase of the frog's litte time to prepare them. There were though three fighte planes, some anti-aircraft gun, about 500 soldiers, etc.
The moment expected arrived... Toad bombe and fighters appeare over Frogington!
O-O-H-
-O-OH-H-E-

Ha! Ha! ya' missed!
But...
I didn't!

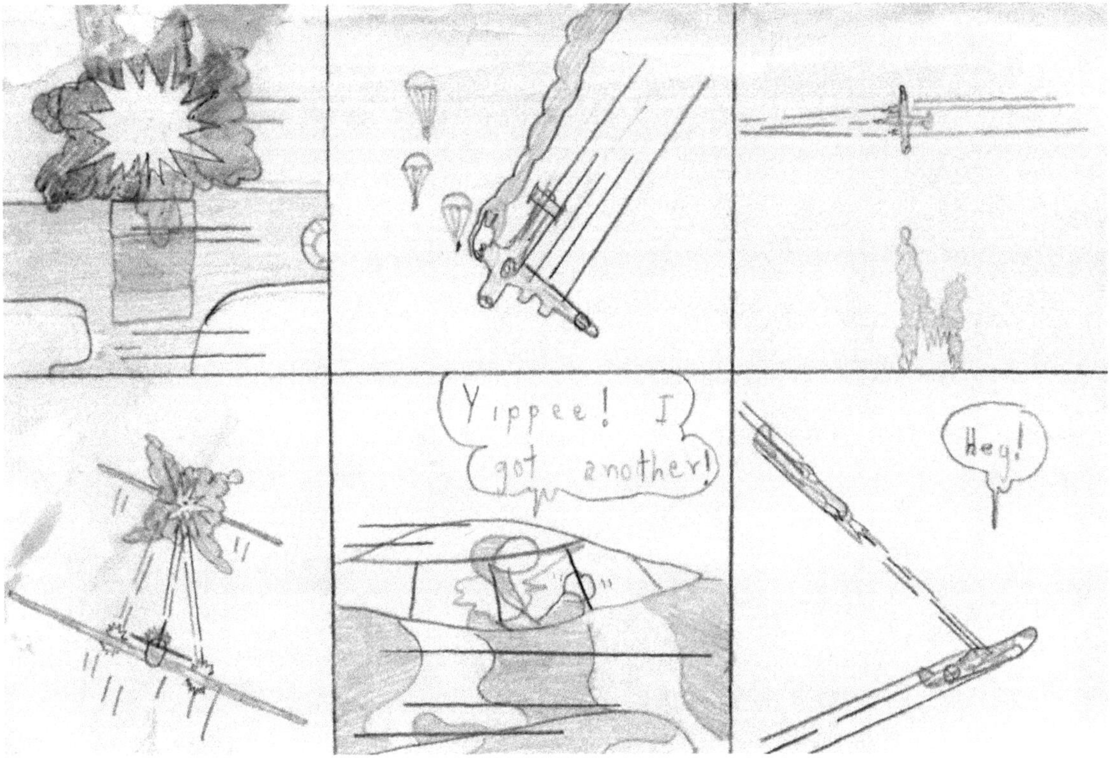
Yippee! I got another!
Hey!

Ill fix that toad for that!

Ah-ha!! He bailing out!
I may get something bad for this, but its worth it...
Oh, I'll hate my self in the morning.
For what I'm doin' today..

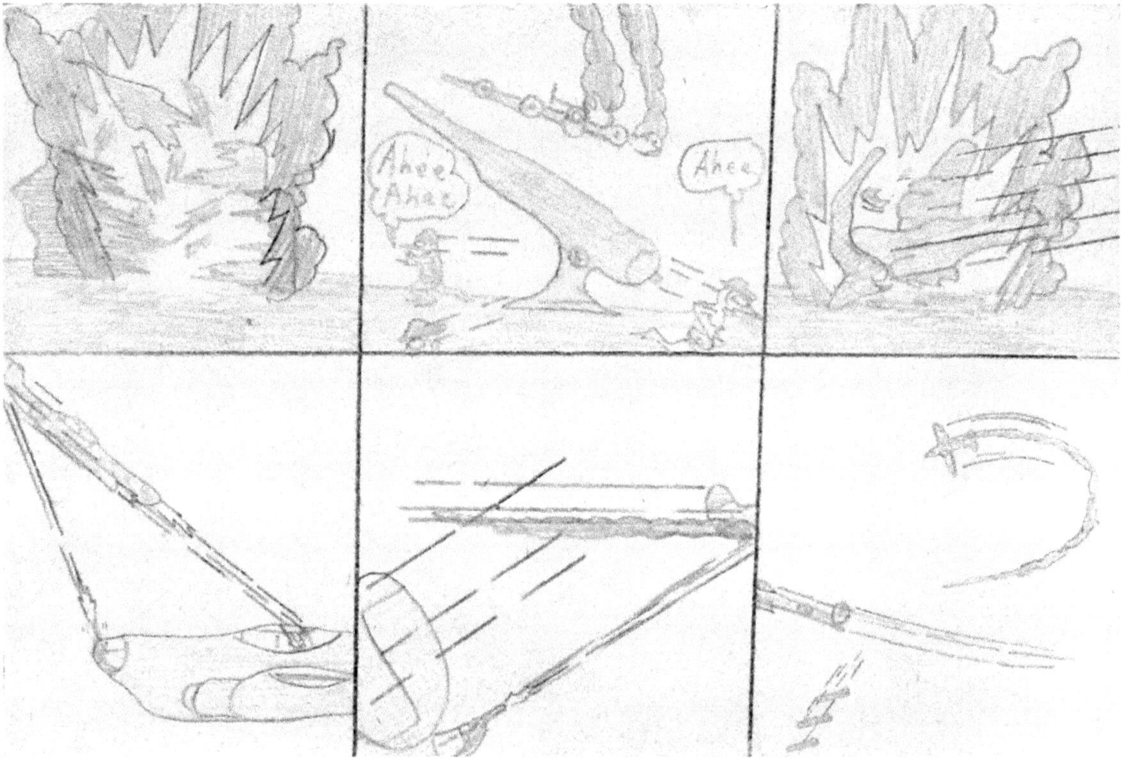
Ahee Ahee
Ahee

Ah-h-gg
got
me!
Aheee

Oh! Oh! I'm the only one left, and YIPE!
I can't let that toad get away with that!
Curse that tricky toad!

What the...
CURSE THAT TRICKY FROG!
S'long
I'll get that cheap frog!
Hey!

All the frog fighters
being down, the
paratroops jump...

Die, Frogs!
This dynamite will fix up some toads!
Now to hold off the toad's till they get it conected up!

yep!
It's all ready!
Hey!
I'll fix those rats, and...

I fix up some of those cheap toads!
The toad fighters now began to strafe.......

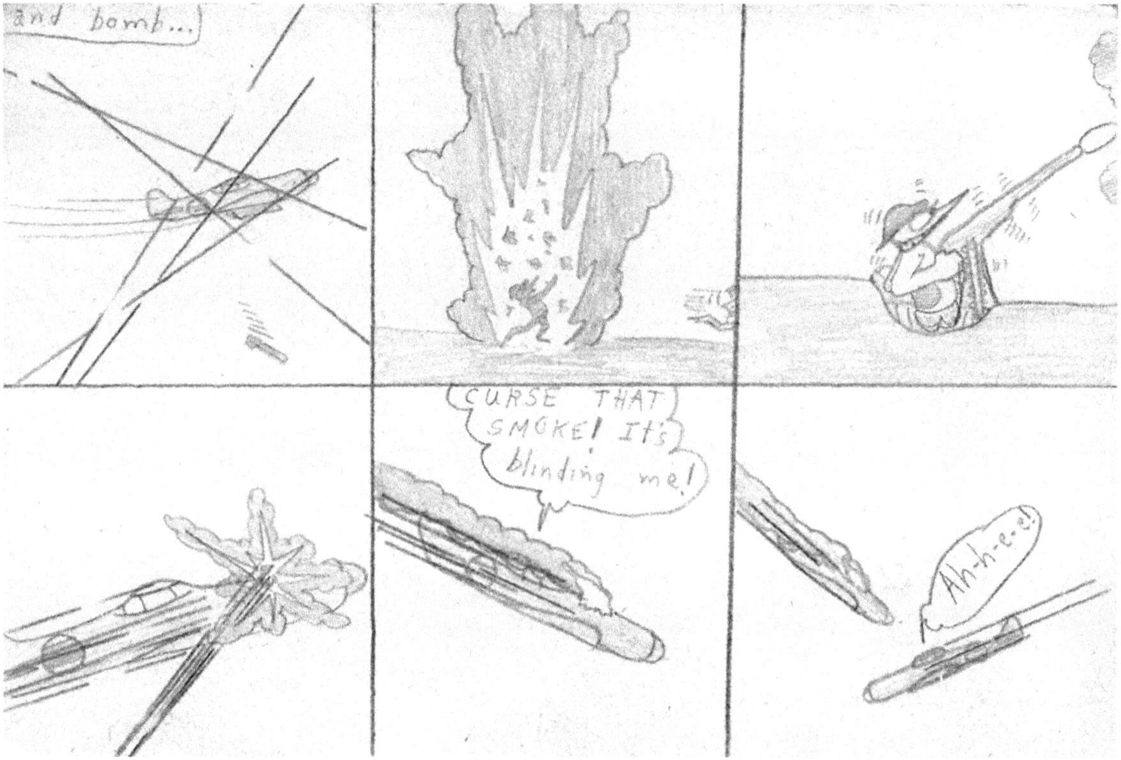
and bomb...
CURSE THAT SMOKE! It's blinding me!
Ah-h-e-e!

While inland a little farther...
Alright men comense firing!
What...
Get back! They're shelling us!

YIPPEE!!!
YIPPEE THEY'VE RETREATED!
But the frog cheered too soon..

Meanwhile...
We've got our big guns now! We'll blow those frogs off the map!
And so...
Frogington...
Was...
finally...
Fairvew Apts.
DESTROYED.

Chapter 3

The Fate of a Toad Convoy

We come upon Toads for the first time not in combat, but simply talking. And we learn that, unlike the Frog archipelago, the Toads live on a "mainland" within striking distance of their enemy. Late at night, the Toads calmly plan their first naval assault, against Eagle Island, to capture it as a base for future raids. No POWs; no negotiation; just modest plans for "bombing and killing all the Frogs." But a Frog spy radios those plans to superiors. Soon, the Frog air force has launched and, by luck, locates the Toad convoy. The air and sea battle begins,

Comic action narration, like combat movies, compresses time so the audience can avoid the boring bits in between. The art does most of the talking. Brief exposition ribbons, like fortune cookie wisdom, guide the action. You are halfway through this chapter before any characters really speak, and then in exchanges between Frog and Toad pilots. Like keeping score at an athletic contest, Jimmy updates the battle's progress with tally sheets. The story is a rapid interchange of duels between planes and between planes and ships, mediated with brief scenes of conversation, offering some "human" drama to the conflict. Jimmy clearly liked the cinematic framing of ships and planes seen from above through cloud breaks. He calculates the Frog victory entirely in the numbers of Toad ships and planes destroyed. Nothing about what victory has cost the Frogs; nothing about lost Frogs.

The fortunate discovery of a Japanese fleet parallels a similar key scene in the 1942 movie *Air Force*. But Jimmy might have known of the March 2–4, 1943, American attack on a Japanese convoy. The Battle of the Bismarck Sea began when a squadron of B-17s saw eight vessels through a window in cloud cover. Sinking four of them immediately, over one hundred planes, including Australian forces, repeatedly struck the convoy over the next two days. US forces also sank twenty-two ships. The story also could have been inspired by the costly US victory over a Japanese invasion force at Midway in June 1942.

Jimmy seemed to enjoy the geometry of converging lines of tracer fire, contrails, and motion lines. The frames are a kind of blueprint of combat concussions. There is no "Kapow!" or "Karang!" of battle onomatopoeia. The rapid pace of fighting and depiction of torpedo bombers hitting ships are also reminiscent of battle scenes in Disney's animated propaganda film *Victory Through Air Power*. Frog bombers seem on the smaller side, with dual wing-mounted engines, belly doors and nose guns, and a single tail. Yet they operate like fighters or perhaps more like Japan's Mitsubishi Ki-21 ("Sally") bomber. Frog fighters have the torpedoes stowed on their bellies like the Grumman Avenger or the Douglas Devastator. But none of Jimmy's planes seem as distinctive as the Curtiss P-40 Warhawk or Lockheed P-38 Lightning. Any erasing he did was primarily to revise dialogue. He switched at times from lowercase lettering to uppercase, a sign of editing indifference. Throughout his comic narratives, Jimmy stuck to the six-panel format. But on page ten of the story depicting a fighter-bomber attacking a Toad tanker, Jimmy began with his typical six-frame layout, later deciding to devote two frames to the fighter diving into the exploding tanker. In the next panel, erasures suggest that he extended the scale of the central flaring explosion.

THE FATE OF A TOAD CONVOY
IN a harbor on the Toad mainland...
The ships are loaded ready to leave, sir!
That's good!!
When these ships reach Eagle Island, we can bomb and kill all the frogs in Frogville, so we must ship the supplies now, at night!!
But...
Certain people will be glad to hear of this...
Now to radio the frog authorities!!

About a half an hour after radioing...
Morning: they reach the convoy...
FROG PLANES!

LOOK! A carrier... Let's go get it!!!

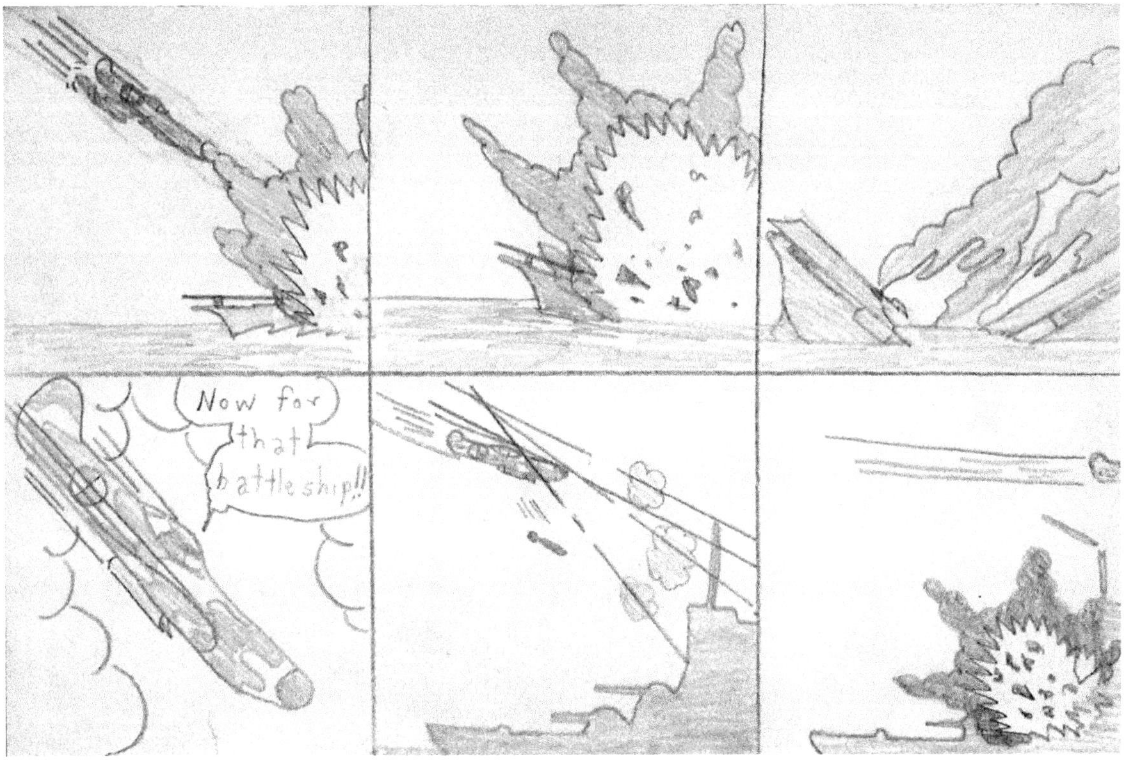
Now for that battleship!!

While...

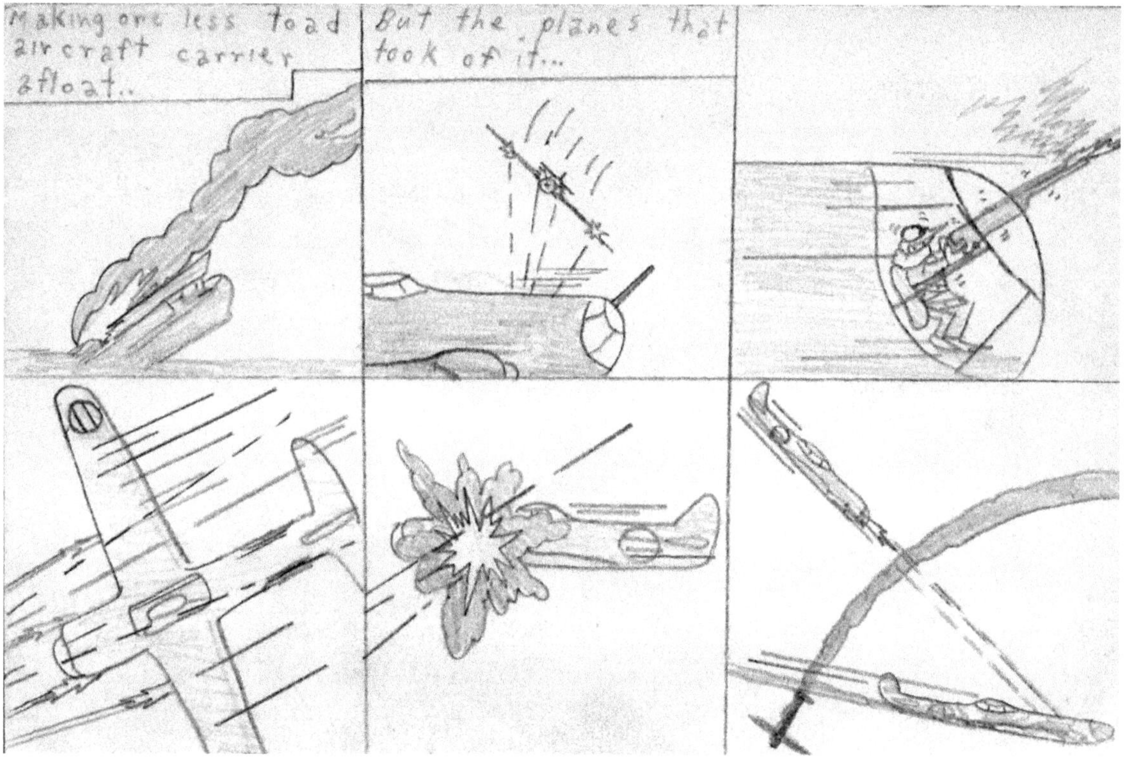
Making one less toad aircraft carrier afloat..
But the planes that took of it...

SO ENDS ANOTHER
TANKER

Now for the other one!!!
HA! HA!
Now where did that frog go? wha.....!!

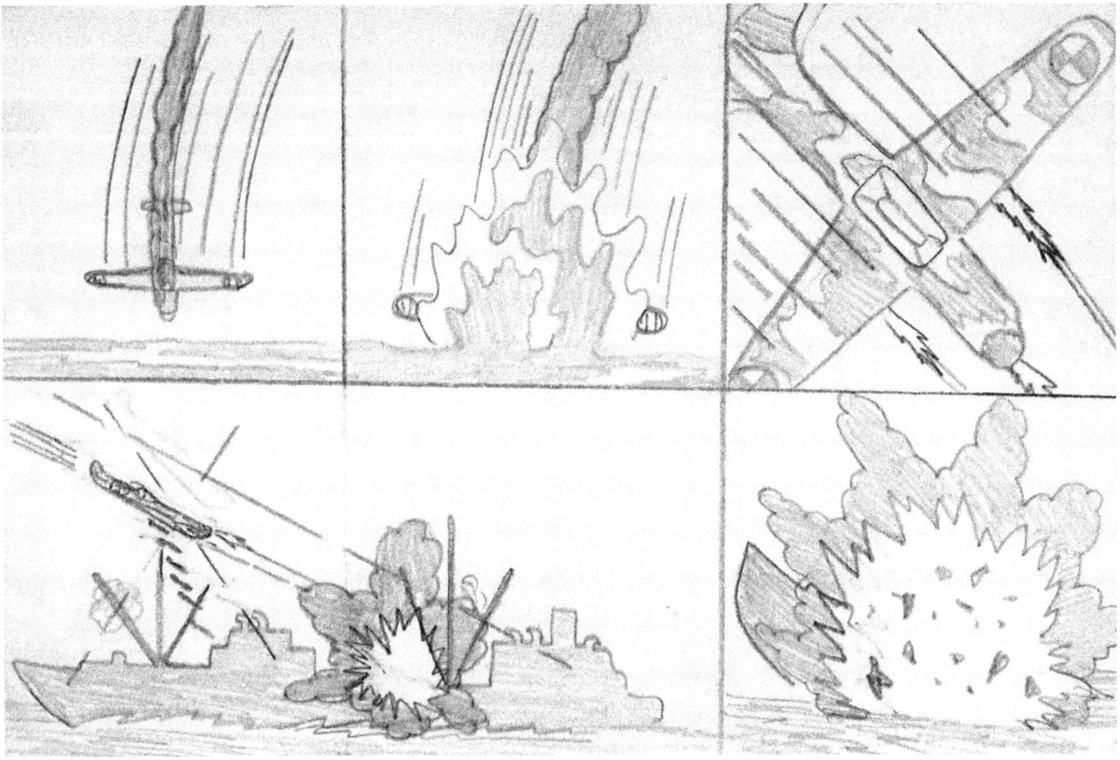

This time we'll get that crazy frog!!

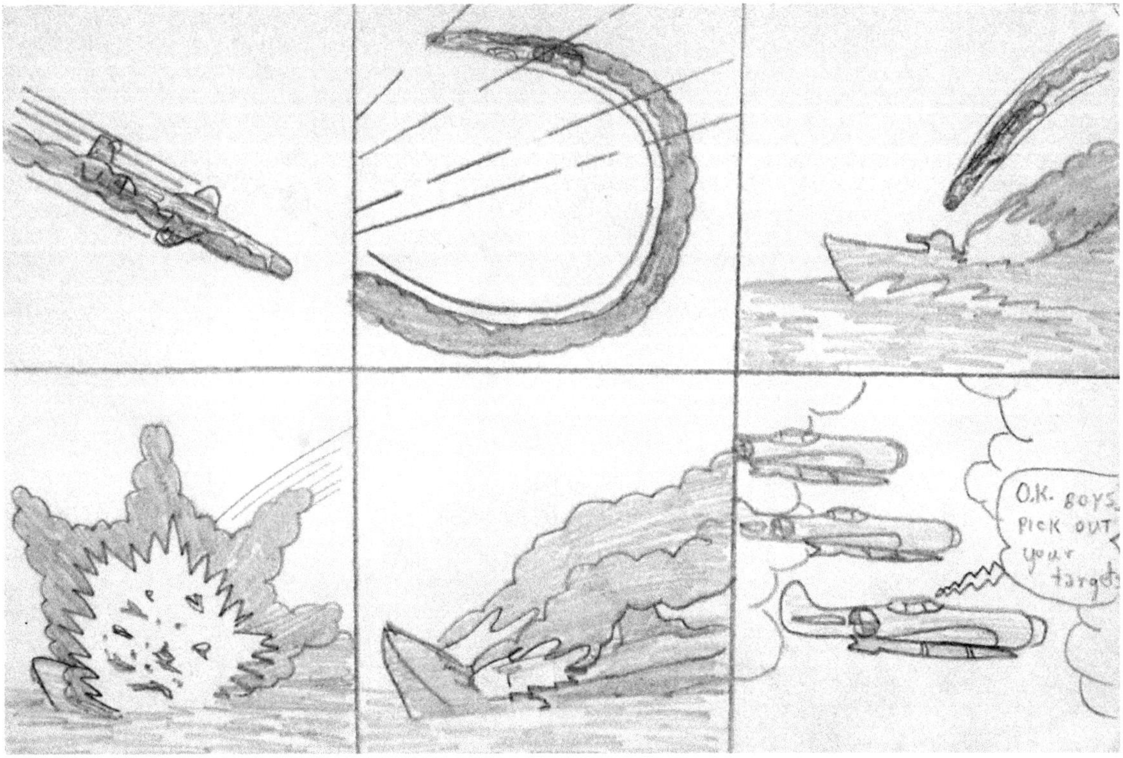
O.K. goys
PICK OUT
your
targ

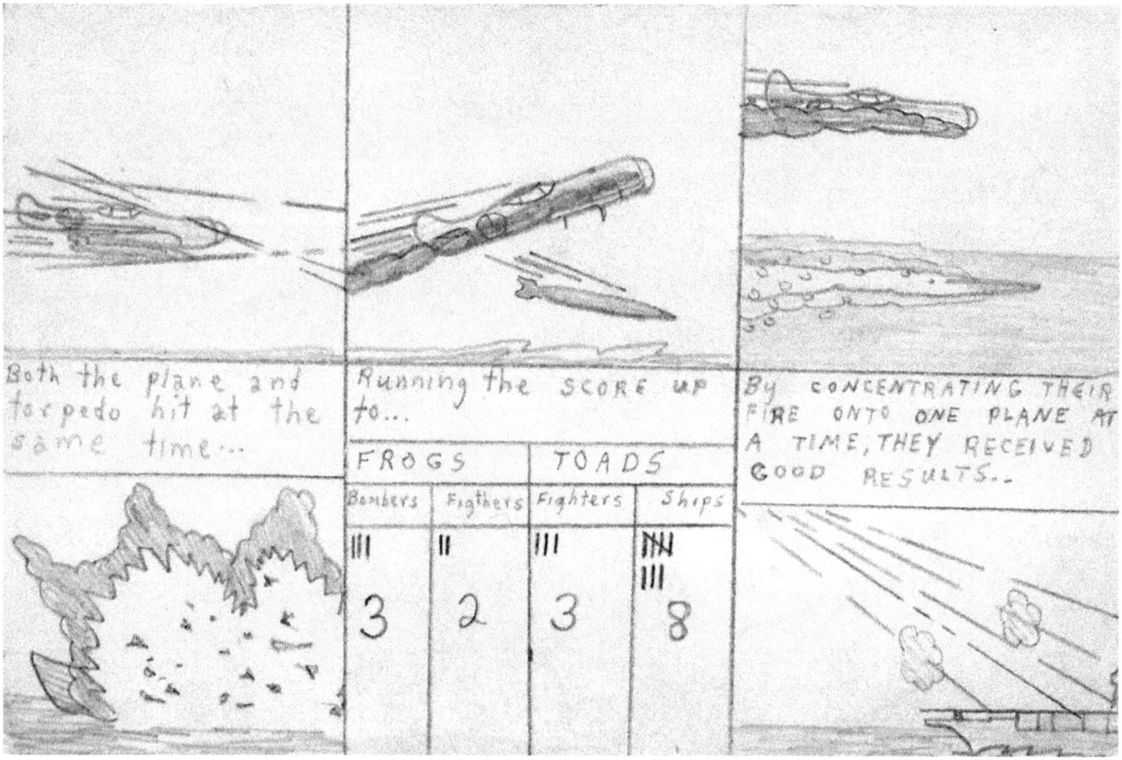
Both the plane and torpedo hit at the same time...
Running the SCORE UP to...
FROGS
TOADS
Bombers
Figthers
Fighters
Ships
3
2
3
8
By CONCENTRATING THEIR FIRE ONTO ONE PLANE AT A TIME, THEY RECEIVED GOOD RESULTS..

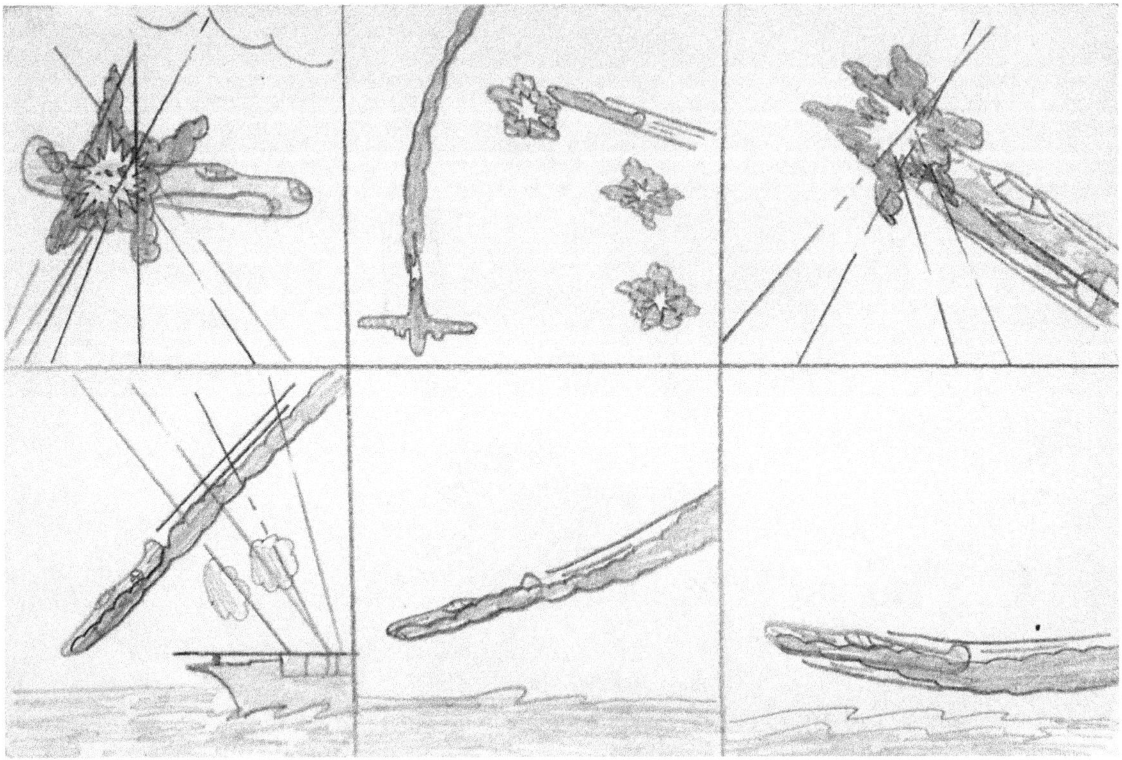

Get the planes off the deck!!
And so while the fighters of both sides battle......

the frog bombers continue to bomb...
the toad convoy!
The score up to now...
FROGS
TOADS
Bombers
Fighters
Fighters
Ships
4
4
4
10
Captain! Look over there!
It's our relief!
And so while the one group of planes speed home...

The newy arrived take up the battle!!!
But that is not all that is coming
Ahee! Frog ships We are lost!

Not being able to pass the frog ships, the toad ships turn around and head for home!!!
The frogs follow and between ships.
And planes sink many more ships.
But unfortunely fog closes in allowing the rest of the ships to escape.
So the planes fly home, with a victory for the frogs!!
FROGS
TOADS
Fighters
Bombers
Ships
Fighters
12
14
15
THE END

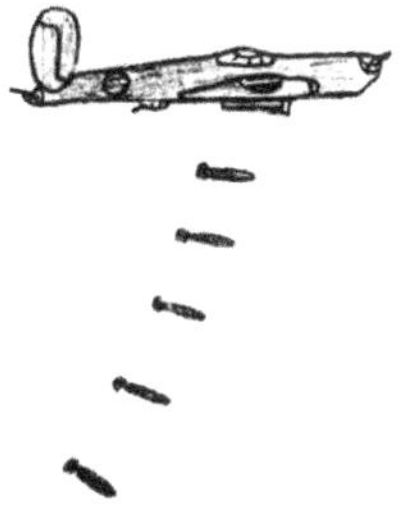

Chapter 4

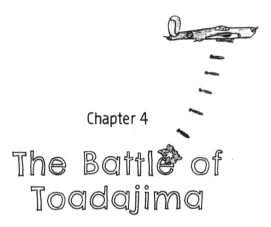

The Battle of Toadajima

This chapter's splash page suggests it will be the most dramatic, perhaps decisive, battle of the war. Only here does Jimmy give two entire panels in capital letters to written exposition. The indications of erasure suggest he reworked his initial plans for the opening, possibly beginning with a conversation as he did in "The Fate of a Toad Convoy." But he finally decided on a dramatic contrast of the battle's importance to its modest setting on "the little island called Toadajima."

Here, Frogs take the war to the Toads. The exposition explains the island's strategic importance. From Toadajima, both the Toad mainland and Eagle Island were within striking range, suggesting that Eagle Island was a Toad possession. Had the Frogs taken Eagle Island early in the war, only to see the Toads retake it? "The Fate of a Toad Convoy" suggests that "Frogville" is on Eagle Island. Again, the chronology and geography are confusing.

Still, Jimmy's naming and depiction of the broad outlines of the battle tell us that the unfinished "Fall of Toadajima" recalled the

American landing on Iwo Jima in February 1945. This tiny volcanic island is about 750 miles south of Tokyo; throughout 1944, a Japanese airbase there sent fighters to harass American bombing runs on Japan. The Marine landing on the island and the month of brutal combat resulted in almost six thousand US deaths and over twenty thousand casualties. The eighteen thousand Japanese troops fought ruthlessly. Just over two hundred were captured, testifying to the merciless struggle.

While the earlier fighting on Peleliu (September–November 1944) was at least as awful, Iwo Jima remains perhaps the best known of the war's island battles. By 1945, the US government had lifted some censorship standards, freeing official newsreels to depict far more combat as well as American wounded and dead. The government also released news of Japanese atrocities against Allied POWs on Bataan. Some evidence of the viciousness with which American troops met Japanese resistance appeared in the press. But US propaganda had long portrayed the Japanese as a treacherous enemy, a militaristic armed mass, and individually as sadistic killers. Primed by such images, Americans may not have been surprised by reports of brutal Japanese resistance.

Jimmy's chapter follows the outline of the actual battle. The Toad installation includes an oil refinery, submarine base, and airstrip that must be captured before invading the nearby Toad homeland. For this chapter, Jimmy borrowed from newsreels and wartime films for tactical explanations and maps. The POV shifts from the sea to the air and land as bomber pilots strafe the refinery and Toad antiaircraft units. The drama focuses on individuals, first as a pilot bails from his stricken plane and then as another pilot must crash-land. The first instance gives us the jungle conflict between the intrepid pilot and a Toad squad. The second one shifts the action to the grass-covered plains where the Frog infantry faces entrenched Toad forces. While the initial splash pages depict a submarine firing a torpedo and the mention of a Toad base forecasted underwater drama, Jimmy's unfinished chapter left that promise unfilled.

Jimmy's panels evoke cinematic combat scenes. His naval forces are relatively idealized silhouettes lit by big, blazing guns. The struggle of the bombers against antiaircraft guns has all the air athleticism of a broken-field halfback. But the chapter's center is the jungle struggle of the lone pilot against a Toad squad. Nearly murdered in cold blood by a Toad ground soldier (drama depicted in the 1942 *Flying Tigers* and 1943's *Air Force*), the pilot, with guile and agility, holds off over a half dozen Toad soldiers who will not take prisoners. The jungle obscures the action, heightening suspense and demanding stealth. The deathly stillness breaks when the snap of a dry branch gives away the pilot's position. Shooting descends, of course, into hand-to-hand combat, the Frog airman finally strangling his Toad combatant, interestingly named "Hans." Cruel vengeance drives both sides, quite literally "the law of the jungle." Without saying so, Jimmy's lone Frog combatant decides to take as many of the enemy with him as possible, recalling not a superhero but the desperation of many a war movie soldier.

The action then shifts to the savanna. There, the hidden threat of Toad gun placements and troops suggests the dug-in character of the Japanese on Iwo Jima and other islands. Single combat again characterizes these scenes. Frog troops toss grenade after grenade into pillboxes and caves. Flamethrowers engulf Toads in burning agony. Throughout, the combatants exchange insults, sarcasm, and cruel humor. These dramatizations of combat, such as the enemy's inhumanity and treachery and the gallows humor of Frog determination, all framed as a visual spectacle, were common in war movies *like Manila Calling* (1942), *Guadalcanal Diary* (1943), *Bataan* (1943),

Objective, Burma! (1945), *The Story of G.I. Joe* (1945), and numerous combat comics.

It isn't clear why Jimmy left "The Fall of Toadajima" unfinished; he lined another six panels. It may well be that he achieved his goals of depicting the different confrontations of naval, aerial, and land engagements with no deep need to conclude the story. The title suggests a Frog victory, unlike the tragic outcomes of the other battles. Perhaps Frog success was less interesting than the emotional payoff from the gallant but futile Frog defenses.

THE BATTLE OF
TOADAJIMA

"TOADAJIMA, ONLY 600 MILES FROM THE TOAD MAINLAND WAS A SUBMARINE BASE AND AN OIL REFINERY TO THE TOADS OF GREAT IMPORTANCE! THE FROG MILITARY STAFT HAD DECIDED TO TAKE THIS ISLAND
BEFORE EAGLE ISLAND AND OTHERS, SINCE FROM HERE BOTH THE TOAD MAINLAND AND EAGLE ISLAND COULD BE READILY BOMBED SO ONE MORNING A PART OF THE FROG FLEET SAILED UP TO...
THE little island called Toadajima...
AND THEY ARE FOUND SHELLING THE BEACH...
TRACERS ALSO POUNDED THE BEACH-
But the toads also had guns....

MANY SHIPS WERE HIT..
Planes rose off carriers to bomb and strafe the island..
but even as they rose, toad planes on the island rose to do battle..
Alright men, strafe the airport!
And so..

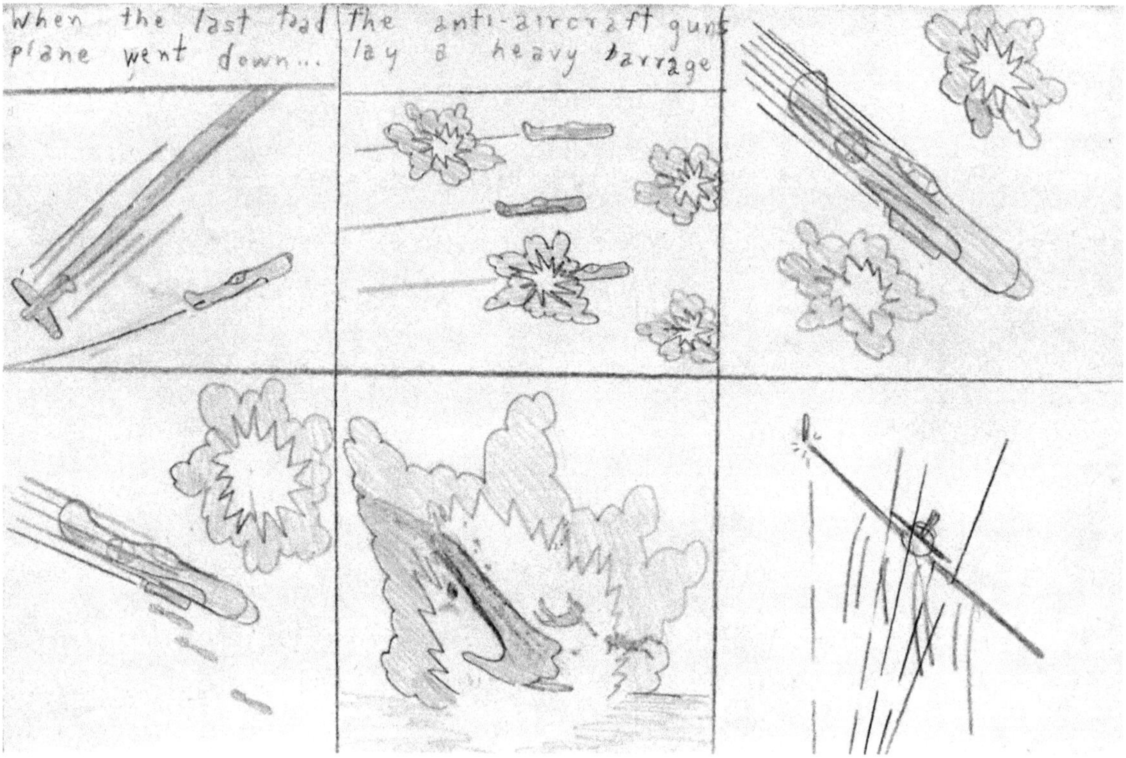
When the last toad plane went down...
The anti-aircraft guns lay a heavy barrage

Shoot down
those plane
before the
ruin our
airport.

Curse the luck! shot down already!
Aha! A frog aviator, helpless too!

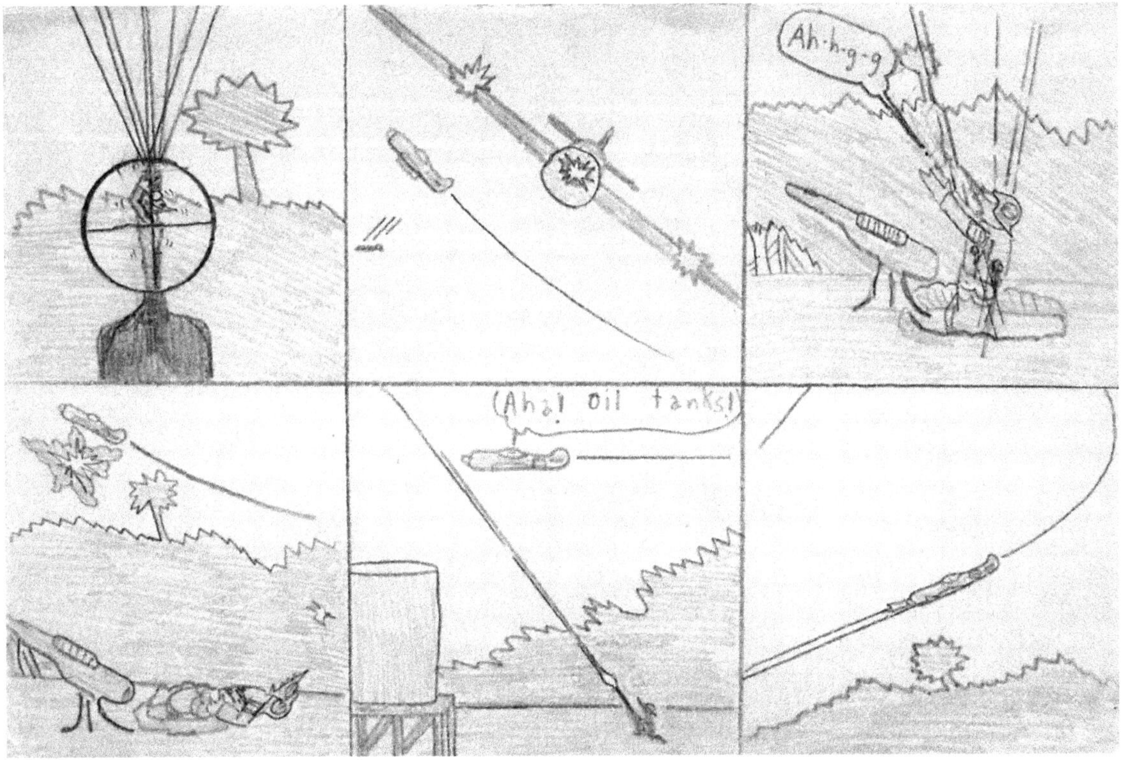
Ah-h-g-g
(Aha! Oil tanks!)

Don't let that frog destroy our oil tanks!

Meanwhile, the frog who had parachuted...
Hope I don't run onto any toads!
CRACK
Who goes there?
Oh! Oh!
I sure I heard a noise back here!
H-m-m, a frog aviator was shot down around here!
Ah-g-gg-

Wonder where Hans went? Oh well.. shots!
Should'nt be any frogs on the island already.. Aha! Put up your hands Frog!
I'll enjoy doing this!
But at that moment
BAM
BOOM
What?

OOF!
Heh Heh Heh
Why you, you...
Now we're even you rat!
From me to you!

Now to finish you!
GASP GASP
That how I treat rats like him!
HALT FROG!
YIPE!
Aha! the toad's machine gun!!

what th-
Ah-h-g-g
Show him no mercy, he has
Killed seven toads
I will show him none, sir!
OOOOH... I'm wounded
OOOH, OOOH

I told you I'd get him!
Sez you! I ought to get all of em' this way!
And he did get all of them...
But one..

At that moment, in the air...
on the sea...
But as the barges neared shore, batteries untouched by the bombing and shelling began to apear...

And in this manner
Five barges were
destroyed..
But most of the toad
guns were destroyed
too!
The first barge landed
to meet...
whithering machine
gun fire!!

But one by one, the machine gun nests are wiped out!!
Although many frogs are killed doing it...
There were many toads hidden in caves
Alright toads! Come out or be burned out!
This is our answer!

And this is my answer!
Ah-h-h-
Aheee
Toads were killed in other caves like this:
While up ahead...

A frog is charging!! Get out the machine gun!!
out goes the machine gun and...
Out goes the frog!

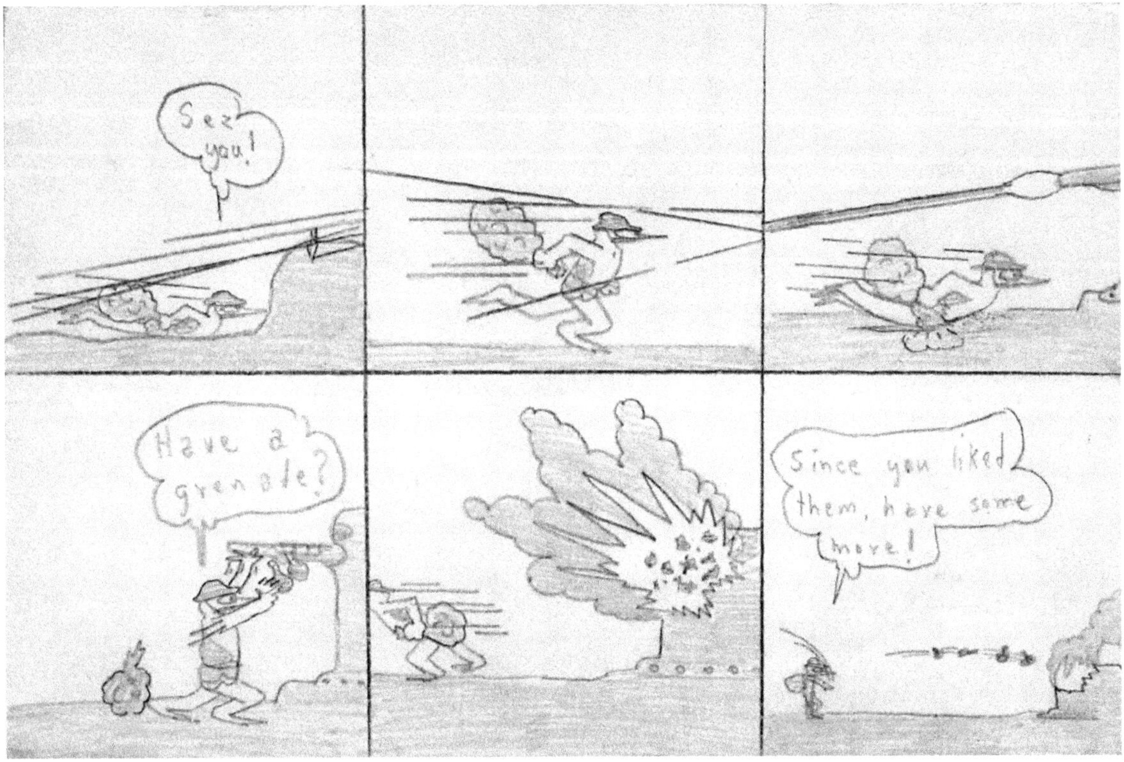
Sez you!
Have a grenade?
Since you liked them, have some more!

Oh! Oh! tall grass!
Bet there's toads in there!
Heh Heh Right you are!

Well, Let's not waste time talkin'! There's toads to be got!
There's one way to solve such a problem!
AH-H-H

AH-H-H-H
While...
So I'm to drop these belly tank bombs on the toads hiding in that tall grass am I?
Well I better follow orders or I might get fired!
Ah-h-h!
Ah-h-h!
Ah-h-h!

Shoot that crazy frog down before he kills us all!
What in... where did that gun come from?

Now I'll finish by strafing this tall grass!
Oh! Oh! I knew it The engine conked out!
CHUG SPUT
Here's hoping!

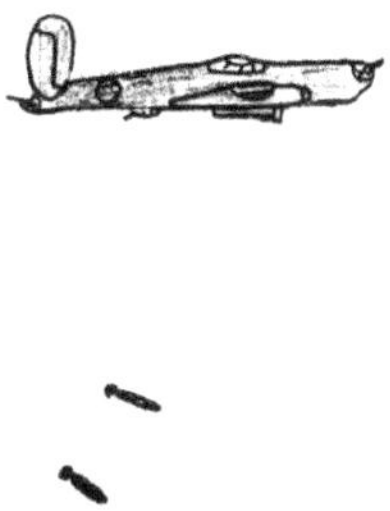

Chapter 5

The Fall of Eagle Island

The longest of the chapters has no splash page. As with "The Fall of Frogington," the Toad air attack bursts out of "a fine day in May." Again, Eagle Island will be a courageous though total defeat for the Frogs, echoing much of the first several months of the US's struggles in the Pacific. Erasing on the first page suggests that the story began with a different title or began as a different story. Similar air combat occurs as earlier. Here, Toad bombers have four engines and a twin tail, similar to the B-24 Liberator, Britain's Lancaster, or the German Ju 390. Both Frog and Toad fighter planes seem to have a single pilot. In one scene, the pilot abandons his stricken plane through a sliding canopy, closest in design to the Republic P-47 Thunderbolt. Toad fighters seem to have a stockier nose, more like the Mitsubishi A6M/ Zero or the Grumman F6F Hellcat. Frog fighters seem to have the narrowed fuselage from the undercarriage toward the nose and propeller of the P-51 Mustang, British Spitfire, or ME 109. Frog fighters are also camouflaged.

The threat of another Toad strafing a helpless, parachuted Frog pilot is interrupted by a Frog pilot killing the pitiless Toad. Toads continue their vicious targeting of civilians, this time bombing a hospital. Some erasure reveals that Jimmy rethought his typical six-frame-per-page format, opting instead for a longer frame that let him dramatize a larger vista of Frog planes at one end watching Toad pilots driven into retreat. The transition permits Jimmy to briefly depict Frogs retrieving the dead and wounded from their wrecked buildings—the only sentimental gesture since the opening chapter. But only briefly. The Toads return the next day in numbers.

As in "Frogington," this attack brings Toad paratroopers, and the action shifts to the ground war. Toad officers wield swords to lead their attack, a reference to Japan's samurai tradition (or perhaps even the US Civil War). However outdated they are by the Second World War, swords are cool. Jimmy's portrait of the attack places Toads in the foreground, where a single boot of one advancing soldier is seen. As in "Toadajima," Jimmy ramps up the banter and caustic humor. The depictions of Frogs and Toads seem sharper, more confident, too. There's another longer frame where a Frog gunner, out of ammunition, faces a Toad bearing down on him. Rifles, machine guns, pistols, knives, bazookas, or tanks rarely miss their targets. The Toad tanks are closest to Shermans, but not Russian or German tanks. The usual bravado prevails: guns are kicked from hands, judo throws disarm opponents, rifles become clubs. Here the battle ends with a melee or battle royal, an entire page of multiple encounters, an epic Rube Goldberg machine of fighting that Jimmy would repeat in later comic strips. A soldier stabs or shoots another, unaware of another enemy poised to kill him. The next page shows the victorious Toads raising their flag over Eagle Island, won at a cost of almost twice the dead as the Frogs who died to keep it.

THE FALL OF EAGLE ISLAND
FROGS
TOADS
One fine day in May on Eagle Island.....
PLANES
WHEEEEOOOOOO
Frog fighters! Get them!

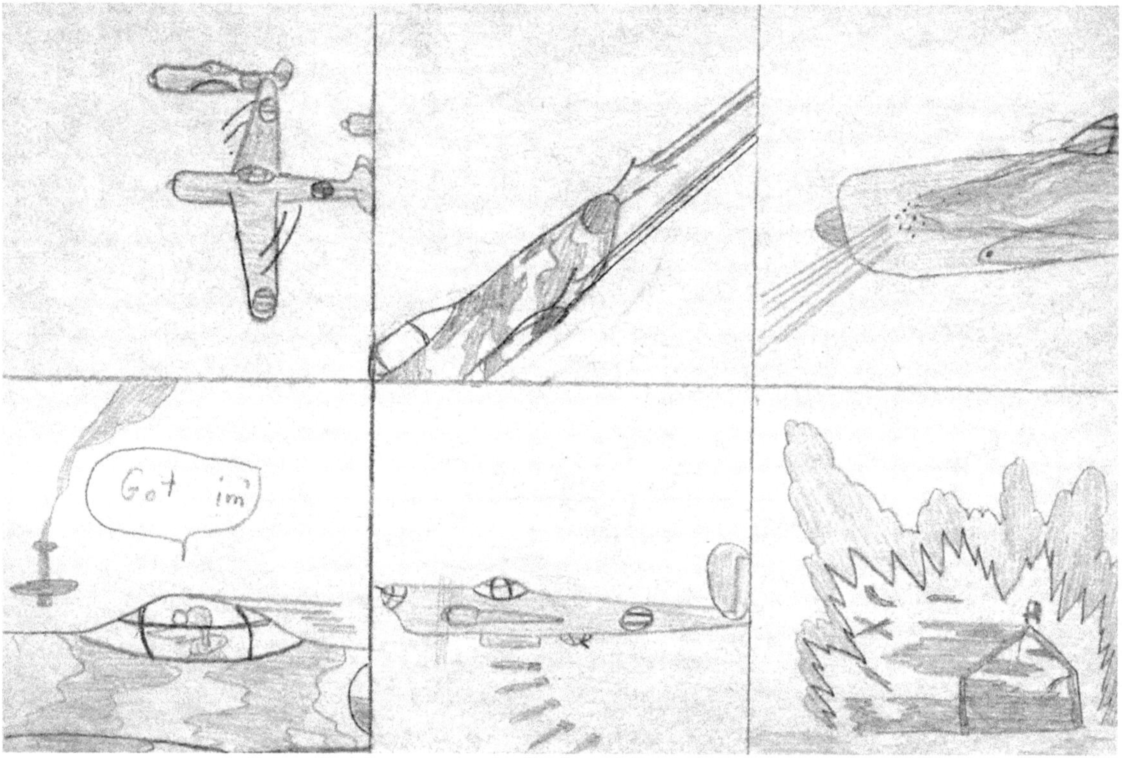
Got im'

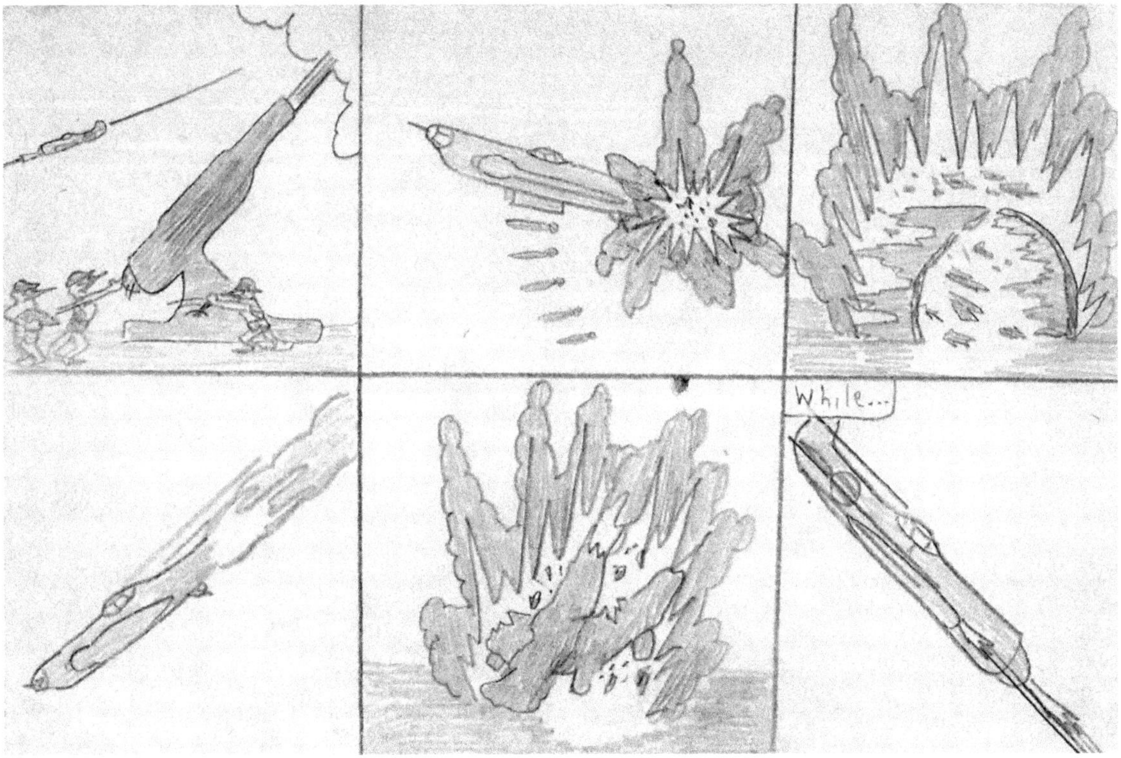
While...

SNAP
!!!!? rudder controls shot away!
There's nothing I like better than helpless frogs!
Oh, no you don't!
*Whe
a gu
has th
closes
shaves
in this
war!

In the bombadier's compartment in one bomber...
Aha!
What is seen through the bombsight..

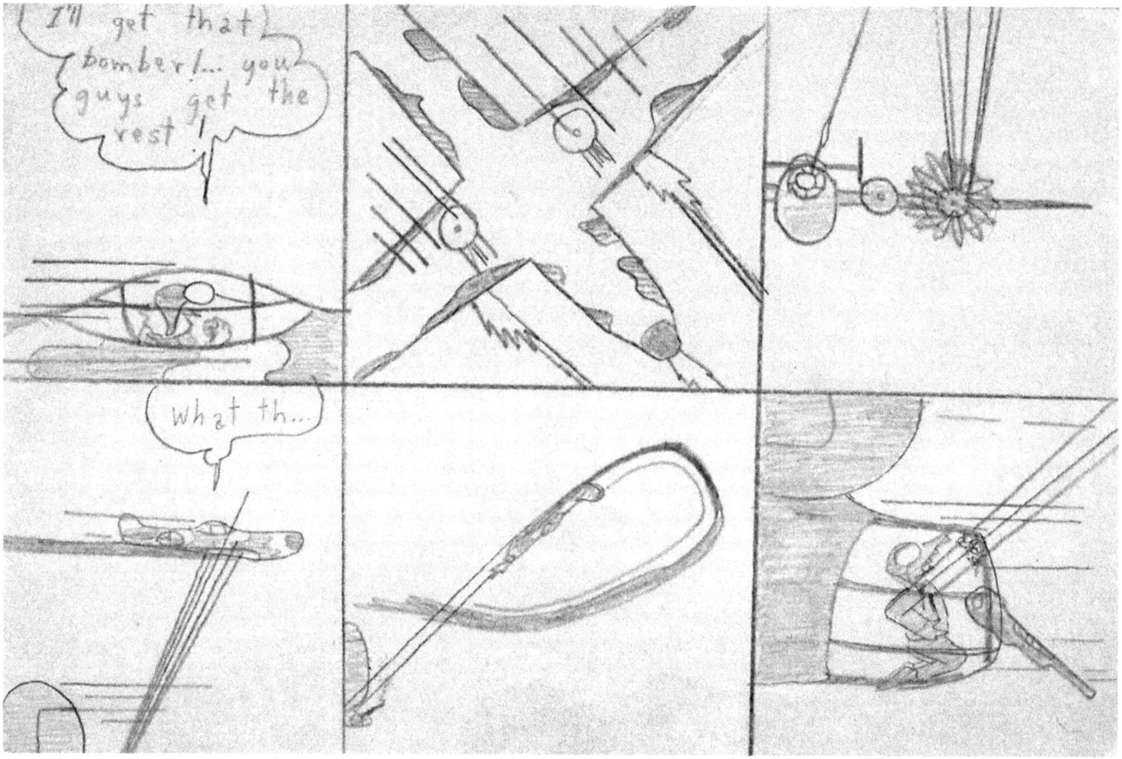
I'll get that bomber!... you guys get the rest!
What th...

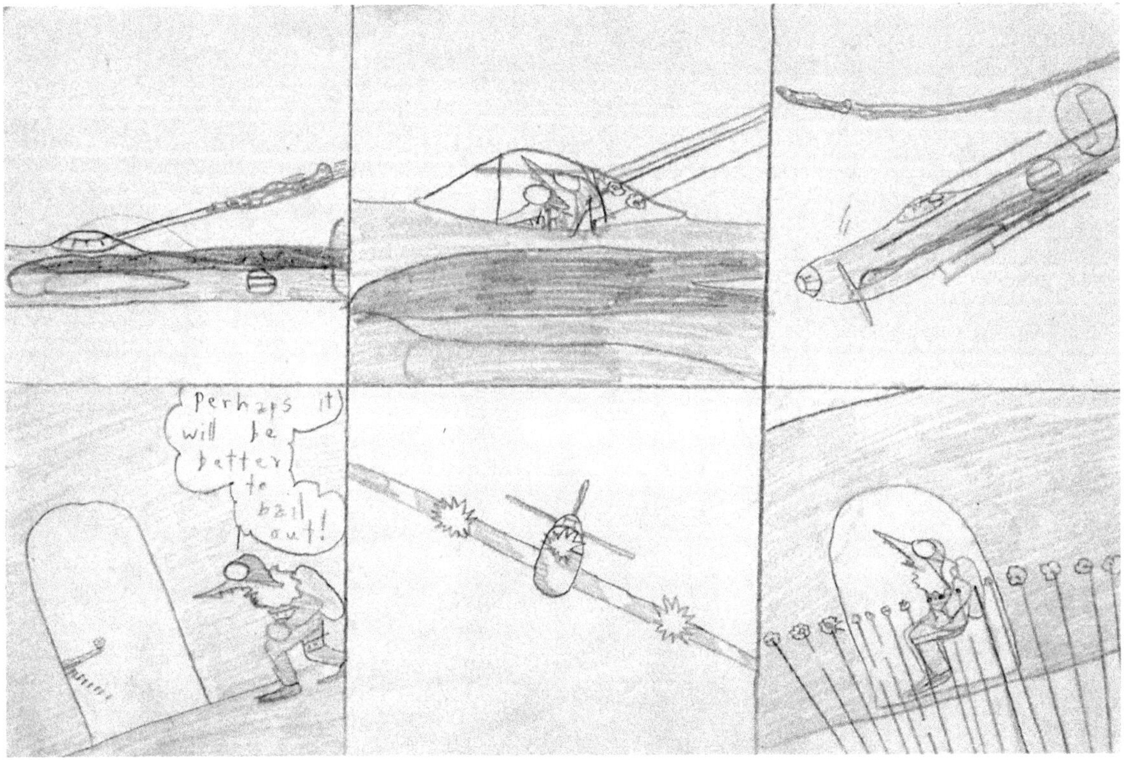
Perhaps it will be better to bail out!

well, thats that No to help the other guys!
But it looks like he needs help himself...
It would be right poor of me, not to avenge that frog.... SO-O-O

Stop the raid and head for the base!
And so the toad planes head for their base, mak
the losses of the frogs two fighters and the losses of the toads four fighters and three bombers.
turn back!

While on Eagle Island
There were many wounded...
And many dead!
But this has just began, for the next day..
HERE THEY COME!!
Up go the remaining two fighters..

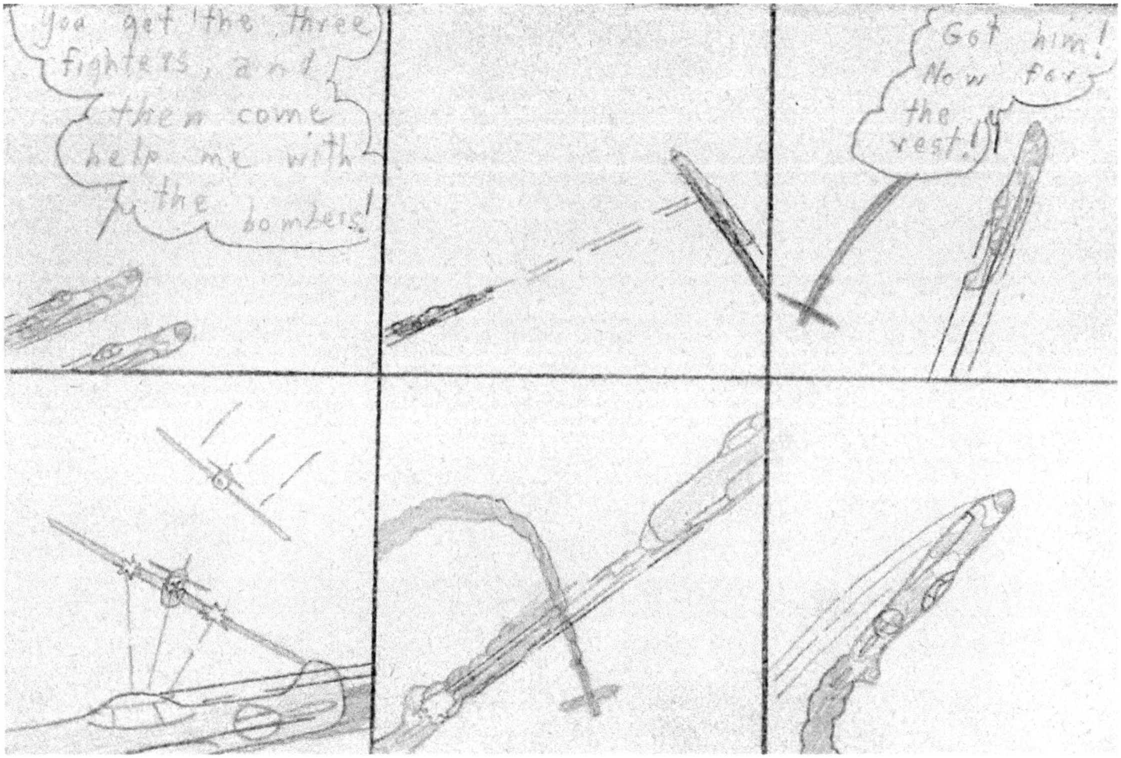
You get the three fighters, and then come help me with the bombers!
Got him! Now for the rest!

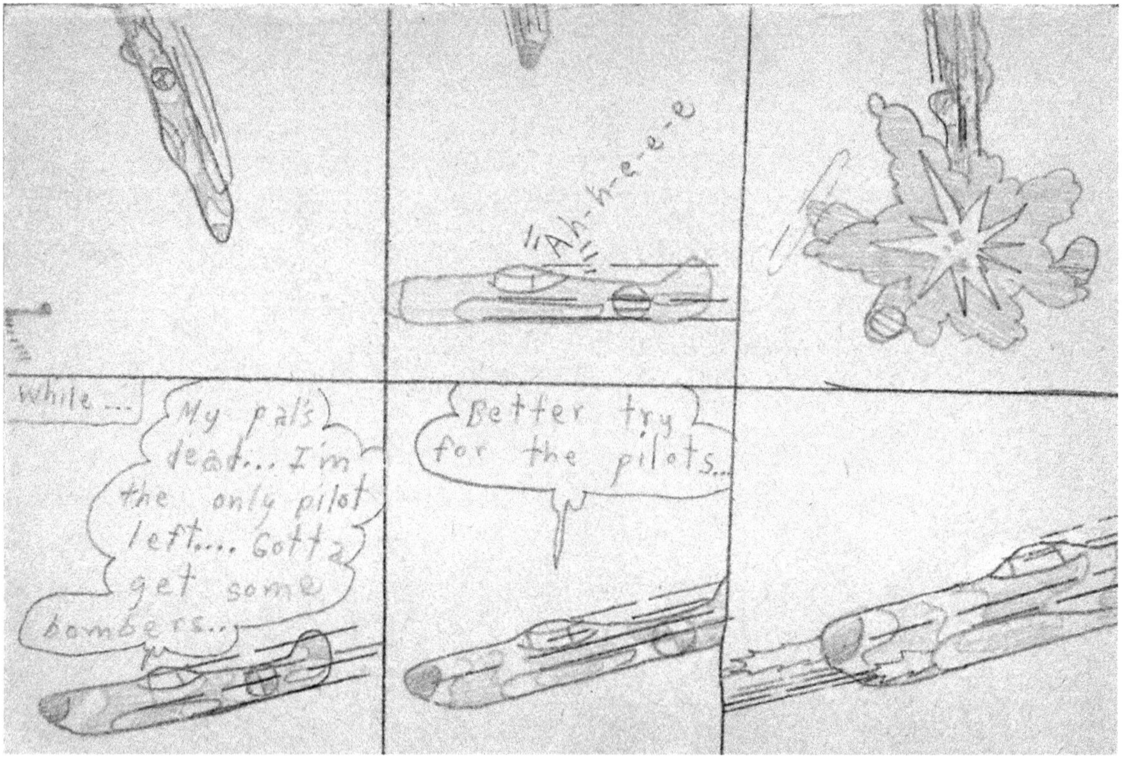
Ah-h-e-e-e
while...
My pal's dead... I'm the only pilot left.... Gotta get some bombers...
Better try for the pilots...

Both the pilot and co-pilot being dead the plane begans to dive...
and crashes...
That's that! Now for another!
CURSES got me!
All the fighters are down now: Let the paratroops jump!

CHARGE!
Wait till those toads come over the hill and.. Ah-h-h.

Greetings!
what th...
Ah-e-e
Thats what you think!
Now you, die Frog OOP

AHH-G-G
WHILE
Ow!
Oh.... I'm wounded..
You don't say!
Now you're dead

Why that filthy toad ... This'll even things up..
CURSES OUTTA' BULLETS
CLICK
Since I don't want it.. they can have it..

Ah-e-e-e
There!
AH-H-G-G
Ah-ha a wounded frog!
This will be easy!

Why you filthy toad!
While at the beach...
Four tanks roll ashore

TANKS! Retreat into the jungle!
The frogs are retreating into the jungle! Follow them!
The tanks are comming! Quick, the bazooka!
Righto!
Righto
Fire!
Kill those frogs!

whew Missed us
Righto
Fire!
CHARGE!

Let em' go!
Into the jungle!
Send a tank after those frogs.
A tank! get ready boys!

What was that...?...I'd better investigate!
Thump
Thats strange! No Frogs here...
Oh no?..
There are no frogs here...
What th...Ah-h-g-g...

got to be careful..
NO!
Seen any Frogs?
What... Ahrg
Then you never will..
After turning this tank around... I go get toads.
Some things wrong! here comes the other tank...
Now I'll keep the tank a rollin', shift into the gun position and...

BLOW UP THAT TANK!
Whew That was close..

Oh-Oh Here come toads!
yes! Too-o-o bad..
LOOK! THE FROG IS DEAD..
Perhaps we had better make sure... give me your knife...
Of course..
This will only take a second..
Sez you..
What th..
Why you..
Hey..

Ah-h-g-g
Put up your hands

Ah-ha-ha-ha-ha
ha-ha...
Ah-ha-ha
Ah-h-g-g...
And now... Ah-ha-
ha-ha-ha-ha-ha
ha-ha-ha-ha-ha-ha-
ha-

TEN THOUSAND CURSES! All our tanks are smashed... CHARGE
Some of em' won't git by me...

STOP THE CHARGE!!
While up about a thousand feet...
I was sent here to machine-gun frogs... now to get down to busines

Run!!
what th..
CURSE THE LUCK!! Hit already!
I'll try again..

Gott'a bail out...

SAFE!
Well well..
?
Hey..

CHARGE!! INTO THE JUNGLE!!
TOADS!

SURRENDER FROG!!
Come and git me!!
Us'ta be a good softball pitcher...!!
yep! still am!!

CHARGE!
Oh!Oh!
CHARGE EM BOYS!!!

As both forces meet, the battle rages...

But finally with all of the 536 frogs who were defending
the islant were dead and 996 of the invading toads dead
the toad flag is raised!

Conclusion

I remember as a child watching *The Wonderful World of Disney* and sitting in awe before images of Disneyland. The fairy castle, the rides and sights on Main Street USA; I was enraptured by those moments. Around that time, I remember thinking, for some reason, about where Disneyland was located. I was so surprised to learn it was in Southern California along the same coast as my hometown of Portland. For some reason, I had believed Disneyland was in New Jersey. Maybe I believed that because I knew New Jersey was so far from Portland, on the other side of the country.

My chances of ever seeing the castle, Mickey, Sleeping Beauty, and the Pirates of the Caribbean were about as good as my chances of traveling to New Jersey. Looking back, I realize my sense of place was captive to my sense of limits. Unlike families on TV, we did not take vacations. We did not travel to remarkable places. We lived paycheck to paycheck. The Canadian novelist Michael Crummey described this state of mind. Discussing his recent *The Innocents*, Crummey wondered about "the appalling confusion" of childhood in a place with limited outside influences, "and then having to try and discover who they were and how the world worked."[1] Kids as imaginative types will turn to creative fantasies to help make sense of a world about which they know so little. They have to build their understanding from a starting point of ignorance. They test that understanding in "what if" situations.

Jimmy Kugler's war was a version of "what if?" creativity about the most exciting and threatening event he knew reimagined in his own terms. In that sense, his war between Frogs and Toads was a form of historical storytelling as "wishful thinking."[2] His comics suggest he knew or cared little about the infrastructure necessary in wartime manufacturing. There is nothing at all about the domestic front past the opening chapter. Still, behind such creative retellings of the past and including reenactments of past events in various forms are compelling desires to experience some significant part of the past in detail. Such interest becomes the closest device we have to a time machine. It carries us in our imaginations, in some cases through the senses of touch, smell, and action into the past through physical re-creations of that world.[3] In so doing, the creative reenactor will filter and mold the evidence of the past according to choices and interests built from contemporary circumstances. In a similar way, Jimmy created, in his comic strip war, a version of the Pacific conflict within a worldview handed down to him through the US media and small-town Nebraska.

There are good reasons to ask if the adolescent comics of one undistinguished kid from a small town who never realized any fame as an artist tell us anything significant about wartime American culture. This question has been put to other stories, ones about "the least of these," so small and insignificant as to encourage us to ignore them. But recovering Jimmy's comics from oblivion and offering a story to help explain them is a kind of redemption. I suggest we owe this to the memory of anyone's life recovered from the debris field left behind by the flood of the past.

At least Jimmy's comics can tell us of the success of American propaganda, of the role of Hollywood and comic book depictions of combat as exciting, as morally straightforward exercises in self-defense and vengeance. The "official" story affirmed the rightness of the cause, while depicting what tremendous adventure war must be. While the war comics portray the justice of the Frog response to the Toad attack, they rarely have a moralistic tone. Not far from government and popular culture depictions of the justice of the American response to Japanese and German aggression, the undeniable justice of the Frogs' cause was the permission to take it to the Toads up to the outer limits of cruelty. Jimmy cared about a comic strip story of an exciting, vengeful war against a treacherous enemy. He cared about aesthetics of dynamic fighting on land and in the air.

In some oblique way, the suffering, anxiety, and privation of the Depression may have opened the way for the war's encouragement of his images and ideas of chaos and fear and violence, too.[4] But much more so, the media portrait of World War II gave Jimmy the authoritative permission to revel in mayhem, brutality, and spectacular destruction. Inaugurating these comics sometime around the end of the war, Jimmy's version of comic strip combat was uninhibited by any qualms about enjoying his own version of warfare as escapist fun, or even a minimal duty to reflect the patriotic aims rife in film and in print. His war said little of patriotism, the inherent virtues of the Frogs; nothing resembling "the American Way."[5] His soldiers express nothing like the dread, despair, or isolation found in the Korean War-era Atlas Comics war stories.[6] His comics exploit the often-overlooked gap between just self-preservation and the voyeuristic desire to see the morbid, the grotesque, and abandoning oneself to the vengeance of a furious crushing of the enemy.

The coverage of the war and his war comic storytelling gave Jimmy a taste for comic depictions of violence he later continued. The comics moved from shooting, explosions, fistfights, and the occasional strangulation and stabbing—with a couple of instances of throat-slitting—to the more grotesque explorations of dark, subversive humor surrounding public torture and cruelty, especially directed against the authorities. Jimmy was able to develop these ideas in the full-scale "Mystery of the Winged Frogs" (fig. 2.1). In the horror genre, the threat often erupts from somewhere in the everyday world, shocking us with terrible violence hidden inside what we take for granted or what we trust. Toad attacks burst out of sunny, peaceful skies. The shock of horror also comes from the threat of the unnatural, as in the case of these comics about murderous Frogs with bat wings.[7] Moving to the violence of the monstrous, Jimmy saw where comic book tastes were evolving from war to crime and horror stories. In the mélange of popular culture, his work helps illustrate how the violence of pre-war and wartime comic art created a taste for the kinds of violence developed in the horror and crime comics popular within a few years of the end of the war.[8]

He later created a range of one-off dark gags where senseless violence shocks us into laughter or intrigues us with the varieties of brutal violence in melee style (figs. 2.2 and 2.3). These interests help explain why Jimmy included no superheroes in his stories.[9] Golden Age superhero comics typically illustrated moralistic storytelling, affirming good citizenship and social order. Even as a vigilante violating the law, the superhero serves authentic justice and decency.[10] During the war, the superhero character easily slipped into patriotic affirmations of the American cause.[11] The violence necessary to restore order and justice before villainous mayhem served those higher causes. Fletcher Hanks's Stardust and Fantomah were exceptions, in tone and violence much closer to Jimmy's fascination with pushing the limits of the comic book art of extreme vengeance.[12]

But before I go too far and exaggerate these comics as aberrant expressions of wartime fascination, I must say again how often Jimmy's comics followed themes and storylines common in both

Figure 2.1 From "The Mystery of the Winged Frogs."

propaganda and popular portraits of the war. Was the enemy ruthless and cruel? Did Americans have to match that cruelty with a relentless killing of equal ferocity? Was the war initially an underdog conflict, characterized by heavy losses, if not defeats, by an unsympathetic mass war machine? Was the invader in some way not quite "human," his victories characterized by stealth, animal cunning if not deceit, by treachery and overwhelming numbers? Jimmy's righteous opponent met Toads with unflinching courage, even desperation, often marked by black humor. His comic strip war was a machine-speed conflict of

Figure 2.2

Figure 2.3

precision materiel, where bombs hit their targets typically in the first pass, and bullets meet their foes with deadly efficiency. Combatants generated a fury of violence necessary to defeat a vicious foe. And yet, the moment that conflict ended, they returned to a normal state of civilian peacefulness. His combatants talked in that unique blend of American slang and references to sports. In these ways and perhaps others, Jimmy's comic strip war was right in the mainstream of official and civilian media portraits.

Nor do I claim that this boy comforted himself with fantasies of violent power to insulate him from the loss, fear, resentment, and loneliness of his childhood. I don't even say that it comforted him before the dullness or petty surveillance he might have resented in a small town. Jimmy apparently made a confession of faith as a Christian at Lexington's First Presbyterian Church in 1944 at age twelve.[13] During the war, First Presbyterian was among other Lexington churches sponsoring a series of lectures on apocalyptic prophecy as a biblical context for the fight against Germany and Japan. Beginning in November of 1943, several evangelists spoke in Lexington on the apocalypse, the "US in End Times" prophecy, the anti-Christ, and biblical plagues.[14] Making a confession of faith and joining a church at age twelve is a singular, serious act. But joining a church that encouraged the kinds of patriotic "End Times" speculations on the war may have given Jimmy even further encouragement in his brand of comic drama.

As Geoff Dyer suggested, comic book landscapes both reflect and shape the reader's imagination; it is mythic, experienced as desire. It is a "mode of narrative imagination." It appears that Jimmy invented a mythic war comic that served him as "extracurricular history."[15] As far as we know, it served him primarily alone. Jimmy Kugler did not intend his late 1940s comic strips for publication. At most, he shared them with his friends and classmates. He drew them, perhaps, as the anti-comic book sentiment reached its pre-Wertham peak among psychologists, educators, and parents. Other members of the helping industry tried to defend comic books for children, at the least to domesticate them, but they met stiff resistance.[16] It is possible Jimmy's teachers frowned on his art, if not discouraged it. With comics as inherently rebellious and considering the scale of this archive, through these stories, Jimmy exercised his independence, if not his anarchist response, to authority.[17] As James Marten suggests about American children in wartime: "They do not simply remain bystanders; nature, desperation, familial and even national loyalty push them to insist on becoming actors in wars large and small. They absorb the politics that lead to war, they exploit the sometimes jarring freedoms offered by wartime, and, as in so many other facets of life, they make the experience their own."[18] Jimmy surely cared deeply about his comic retelling of the war. The comics tell us that he believed his imagined war was real, at least emotionally, to him.

He certainly cared enough about them to hold onto the comics long past high school, carrying them in his moves from Nebraska to Denver to Salt Lake City and eventually to Portland, Oregon. He did not produce them for pay; he did not draw them as an introduction to a career in the arts. They are the reenactments by a history buff, eager to create and tell his own paneled stories, his own reworking of the events, comic art, radio drama, and movie conflict preoccupying his adolescent imagination. His dedication to the craft and perseverance of comic storytelling was his youthful, skilled, imagined conversation with the most fascinating parts of his own mass culture. The comics tell how a Nebraska boy's creative zeal distilled typical rebellion, loneliness, and fascination with the macabre into something dynamic and strange. With these comics, he achieved the dream of a young storytelling artisan inspired to reinvent his own world.

Notes

Introduction

1. As I interpret the war comics, it will be more obvious about when to place the earliest date for certain stories or images. But dating the entire collection suggests a more complex problem. Paul Karasik argues that the war comics represent greater artistic skill and so followed the earlier "Mystery of the Winged Frogs" story; see "Die Frogs! The Lost Comics of James Kugler," *Comics Journal* 307 (Winter/Spring 2021): 212–21. While I should defer to Karasik's artistic experience and scholarly argument, I find the war comics generally less technically accomplished, which I hope to explain as we go.

2. In wartime, educators, national and local leaders, and military officials worried that high rejection rates for inductees represented a national crisis of American male fitness for military service. Propaganda and school activities, especially PE and athletics, reflect increased national attention to student fitness, moral character, hygiene, resilience, and obedience to authority. On such programs, see Christina S. Jarvis, *The Male Body at War: American Masculinity during World War II* (Dekalb: Northern Illinois University Press, 2010), 58–64, 69–72.

3. Paula S. Fass describes the "creation" of the modern high school in which adolescents were under more unbroken adult supervision than before, which helped establish that period of youth as a definitive and critical stage of life. This authority and the accompanying pressure on kids to meet a standard of "normal" meant that school competed with home as the major authority in a kid's life. See *The End of American Childhood: A History of Parenting from Life on the Frontier to the Managed Child* (Princeton: Princeton University Press, 2016), 134, 140–41, 158–60, 162, 168. For the youth "crisis," see James Gilbert, *Cycle of Outrage: America's Reaction to the Juvenile Delinquent in the 1950s* (Oxford: Oxford University Press, 1988), and Grace Palladino, *Teenagers: An American History* (New York: Basic Books, 1997).

4. On children's storytelling, especially the carnivalesque character of their fascination with the forbidden and taboo, see Brian Sutton-Smith's *The Ambiguity of Play* (Cambridge, MA: Harvard University Press, 2001), 121–22, 158–59, 162–63. Sutton-Smith is especially helpful in considering children's play as a serious cultural activity. However, it is not clear where cartoons would fit into his taxonomy of toys and circumstances of play; see for instance p. 228. Philip D. Beidler presents one lively model of studying what he called "postwar remembering," a culture-wide production of books, plays, films, and documents. Soon after 1945, "the Good War" generated its own self-representations and propaganda. See *The Good War's Greatest Hits: World War II and American Remembering* (Atlanta: University of Georgia Press, 1998), 17. But the groundwork for "the Good War" myth was likely laid sooner in the mutual aid of war journalists and military leadership. See Michael C. C. Adams, *The Best War Ever: America and World War II* (Baltimore: Johns Hopkins University Press, 1994).

5. Children leave behind few records. Typically, histories of childhood depend upon the memories of adults about their own childhood and adult witnesses speaking on behalf of children. On this problem see Steven Mintz's "Prologue," *Huck's Raft: A History of American Childhood* (Cambridge, MA: Belknap Press, 2004); Peter N. Sterns, "Challenges in the History of Childhood," *Journal of the History of Childhood and Youth* 1, no. 1 (Winter 2008): 35–42; Paula S. Fass, "Childhood and Memory," *Journal of the History of Childhood and Youth* 3, no. 2 (Spring 2010): 155–64. In the opinion of Henry Jenkins, the child's identity in history often finds itself expressed between adult desire and the child's fantasies: introduction to *The Children's Culture Reader*, ed. Henry Jenkins (New York: New York University Press, 1998), 25. Evidence of early artistic creativity comes from authors whose later fame made their childhoods more important: the Brontë family, Jane Austen, and C. S. Lewis come to mind.

6. Some of our most influential creative artists probably followed a similar path. Most comic book artists started out imitating their favorite comic strips. Some of this has survived; see, for example, the interviews in David Hajdu's *The Ten-Cent Plague: The Great Comic Book Scare and How It Changed America* (New York: Picador, 2009). Jack Cole's childhood drawing can be found in Art Spiegelman and Chip Kidd, *Jack Cole and Plastic Man: Forms Stretched to Their Limits* (San Francisco: Chronicle Books, 2001).

7. Emmy E. Werner, *Through the Eyes of Innocents: Children Witness World War II* (Boulder, CO: Westview Press, 2000).

8. Many have rounded edges as if salvaged from the paper backing in pantyhose packages. Others have rough edges, perhaps half of a 12" × 9" plain sheet.

9. The former has part of Frances Miles Finch's (1827–1907) poem "The Blue and the Gray," Leigh Hunt's (1784–1859) "Abou Ben Adhem," and a short passage from Laura Ingalls Wilder's *Little Town on the Prairie* where her mother writes a dedicatory

verse in an autograph album. In the eighth grade, probably in the seventh too, Jimmy and his best friend Jack Kutz frequently got into trouble for drawing Frogs during class; Myrl Sage, telephone interview by author, Lexington, NE, July 30, 2010, written notes, p.1. Another classmate recalled that Jimmy and Kutz passed their cartoons around their high school classes, primarily among their male classmates; Nola (Jones) Reed, telephone interview by author, Orange City, IA, June 3, 2021.

10. Histories of American popular culture can still overlook or pay little heed to comic books. Jim Cullen, in *The Art of Democracy: A Concise History of Popular Culture in the United States*, 2nd ed. (New York: Monthly Review Press, 2002), says nothing about them. Raymond F. Betts and Lyz Bly mention superheroes only in passing; *A History of Popular Culture: More of Everything, Faster and Brighter*, 2nd ed. (London and New York: Routledge, 2013). For "low" culture, I follow Patricia Johnston's careful distinctions on the relationship of "high" and low," though she and her coauthors do not discuss comics; Introduction to *Seeing High and Low: Representing Social Conflict in American Visual Culture*, ed. Johnston (Berkeley: University of California Press, 2006).

11. *The Seven Lively Arts* (New York: Harper and Brothers, 1924), 215.

12. William W. Savage Jr., *Commies, Cowboys, and Jungle Queens: Comic Books and America, 1945–1954* (Middleton, CT: Wesleyan University Press, 1990); Bradford W. Wright, *Comic Book Nation: The Transformation of Youth Culture in America* (Baltimore: Johns Hopkins University Press, 2003); Gerard Jones, *Men of Tomorrow: Geeks, Gangsters, and the Birth of the Comic Book* (New York: Basic Books, 2005); and Jill Lepore, *The Secret History of Wonder Woman* (New York: Vintage Books, 2015).

13. To begin, see Joseph Witek, *Comic Books as History: The Narrative Art of Jack Jackson, Art Spiegelman, and Harvey Pekar* (Jackson: University Press of Mississippi, 1989); on biography and autobiography especially treating the memory of trauma, see Hillary Chute, "'The Shadow of a Past Time': History and Graphic Representation in 'Maus,'" *Twentieth Century Literature* 52, no. 2 (Summer 2006), 199–230; Frederik Byrn Kohlert, "Working It Through: Trauma and Autobiography in Phoebe Gloeckner's *A Child's Life* and *The Diary of a Teenage Girl*," *South Central Review* 32, no. 3 (Fall 2015): 124–42.

14. Matthew Pustz, ed., *Comic Books and American Cultural History: An Anthology* (New York: Continuum, 2012); Trisha Goodnow and James J. Kimble, eds., *The 10 Cent War: Comic Books, Propaganda, and World War II* (Jackson: University Press of Mississippi, 2017); Scott Cord, *Comics and Conflict: Patriotism and Propaganda from WWII through Operation Iraqi Freedom* (Annapolis: Naval Institute Press, 2014).

15. One model for this kind of work, though outside the history of childhood studies, is Michael Moon's careful contextual study of Henry Darger's (1892–1973) epic art, among other things, his interest in Chicago's daily comic strips; *Darger's Resources* (Durham: Duke University Press, 2012). Darger is also interesting as a largely self-taught artist with no desire to share his work with audiences. For a brief introduction

to his life and the scholarship on him, as well as his art in relation to comics, see Gavin Parkinson, "Henry Darger, Comics, and the Graphic Novel Contexts and Appropriations" in *The Cambridge History of the Graphic Novel*, ed. Jan Baetens, Hugo Frey, and Stephen E. Tabachnick (Cambridge: Cambridge University Press, 2018), 139–54.

16. This seems true despite the obvious concerns at the time of educators, psychologists, and cultural gatekeepers about the "problem" of the comic book and American youth. Historians of American childhood do not ignore comics and comic reading. But the several excellent works I mention in the above notes and those to come typically give them little direct attention. Groundbreaking historians of the comic book such as Brad Wright, William Savage, Gerard Jones, and Qiana Whitted say little about the historical circumstances of the child readers of those books. Carol L. Tilley's work on library readership of comics and children's responses to the comic book controversies of the 1950s (cited in notes below), and some of the essays in *The 10 Cent War*, come as close as anyone to combining these diverse fields.

17. Documents associated with "lost peoples" have usually been generated by civil officials, educational authorities, the media, and religious powers. Carlo Ginzburg's primary sources on the miller Menocchio in *The Cheese and the Worms: The Cosmos of a Sixteenth-Century Miller*, trans. John and Anne Tedeschi (Baltimore: Johns Hopkins University Press, 1992), were created by the authorities, not the subject himself. Ginzburg had to shape or interpret those sources in peculiar ways to recover his miller's voice. On this subject see Edward Muir, "Introduction: Observing Trifles," in *Microhistory and the Lost Peoples of Europe*, ed. Edward Muir and Guido Ruggiero (Baltimore: Johns Hopkins University Press, 1991), xvi; Giovanni Levi, "On Microhistory," in *New Perspectives on Historical Writing*, ed. Peter Burke (University Park: Pennsylvania State University Press, 1991), 93–113; and *Small Worlds: Method, Meaning and Narrative in Microhistory*, ed. James F. Brooks, Christopher R. N. DeCorse, and John Walton (Santa Fe: School for Advanced Research Press, 2008).

18. Alongside other studies, I've modeled this project on microhistorical approaches represented especially by Joseph A. Amato, *Rethinking Home: A Case for Writing Local History* (Berkeley: University of California Press, 2002), and Sigurður Gylfi Magnússon, "The Contours of Social History. Microhistory, Postmodernism and Historical Sources," in *Mod nye historier. Rapporter til det 24. Nordiske Historikermøde* 3, ed. Carsten Tag Nielsen, Dorthe Gert Simonsen, and Lene Wul (Århus, 2001); also in *The Contours of Social History—Microhistory, Postmodernism and Historical Sources. Mod nye historier.* Rapporter til Det 24. Nordiske Historikermøde. Vol. 3, ed. Carsten Tage Nielsen, Dorthe Gert Simonsen, and Lene Wul (Århus, 2001), 83–107. Perhaps the version closest to what I imagine accomplishing with the comics is found in Paul Karasik's introduction to Fletcher Hanks's comics, *Turn Loose Our Death Rays and Kill Them All! The Complete Works of Fletcher Hanks* (Seattle: Fantagraphic Books, 2016).

19. David Drozd and Jerry Deichert, "Nebraska Historical Populations: Quick Reference Tables" (University of Nebraska at Omaha: Center of Public Affairs Research, 2018), 31, at https://www.unomaha.edu/college-of-public-affairs-and-community-service/center-for-public-affairs-research/documents/nebraska-historical-population-report-2018.pdf.

20. For the possible difficulties using local newspapers as sources see the selection from Edna Ferber's *A Peculiar Treasure* in *A Place Called Home: Writings on the Midwestern Small Town*, ed. Richard O. Davies, Joseph A. Amato, and David R. Pichaske (St. Paul: Minnesota Historical Society Press, 2003), 185–86.

21. Republicans typically returned big majorities in elections; for example, *The Lexington Clipper* reported on August 18, 1938, that Republicans outvoted Democrats in a recent Dawson County election, 4171 to 1792.

22. The *Lexington Clipper*, March 27 and May 8, 1941 (all subsequent citations as *Clipper*). On the hardships of small midwestern towns even before the Depression see Cheri Register, *Packinghouse Daughter: A Memoir* (St. Paul: Minnesota Historical Society Press, 2001); Davies, Amato, and Pichaske, *A Place Called Home*, 213–14.

23. *Clipper*, December 28, 1939. "A Progressive Community," "one of Nebraska's finest small cities," in *Yellow Pages*, Lexington, Nebraska [telephone directory], 1948, the Nebraska State Historical Society.

24. *Clipper*, March 28, 1940; also May 26, 1938.

25. Amato, *Rethinking Home*, 99.

26. *Clipper*, October 26, 1939, November 16 and 23, 1939.

27. June 8, 1941; August 17, 1939.

28. On war bond drives: *Clipper,* September 23, 1943 and November 4, 1943; on half the local school teachers in the fall being new hires, August 12, 1943.

29. For nearby Buffalo County, see Mark Ellis, "Casualties of War: Buffalo County, Nebraska and Its World War II Dead," *Nebraska History* 101, no. 3 (Fall, 2020): 106–21.

30. *Clipper*, May 21, 1945, "German War Prisoner Died of Heart Attack" while working at the Meyer Milling Company east of Lexington. He had been interned at the Atlanta Camp that opened in 1943. Fort Robinson in eastern Nebraska was the main facility; Grand Island had a satellite installation.

31. There were bases as close as Kearney and Grand Island. Three crashes occurred near the Kearney base: one in Betrand, about twenty miles south of Lexington and one in Wellfleet, about seventy miles west. Jerry Penry, "Nebraska's Fatal Air Crashes of WWII," at http://www.nebraskaaircrash.com/main.html (accessed 6/7/11). A captured German tank, ME 109, and Italian fighter were brought for display as close as Grand Island on August 4–5, 1943; http://www.nebraskaaircrash.com/events/display.html (accessed 6/7/11).

32. On November 18, 1943, the *Clipper* ran a big ad for visiting evangelist J. J. Williamson, Director of the Bible Auditorium of the Air. The week's program included "World's Greatest Criminal: Who Is he? Hitler or Hirohito?"; "Four Mysterious Horsemen Riding through the World: White, Red, Black, and Pale. What do they mean?" On January 6, 1944, evangelist Lyman Shaw was advertised to teach "Seven Terrible Plagues Coming."

33. Obituary of Otto Kugler, *Clipper*, May 6, 1966. Evidence for the work and class experience of typesetters from this period is hard to track down. One author argued that unlike other cases of machine development, the mechanization of printing by the linotype required a high level of skill and concentration. Frank Tracy Carlton, *The History and Problems of Organized Labor* (Boston: D.C. Heath, 1911), 115–16. In New Zealand, operators and typesetters were respected, skilled laborers commanding high wages. They had mixed feelings about the transition from hot type printing to cold type in the 1970s. Some were happy to leave behind the noise and grime of the old linotype machines. Others missed the skill associated with them and found the new technology boring. Peter Franks, *Print and Politics: A History of Trade Unions in the New Zealand Printing Industry, 1865–1995* (Wellington: Victoria University Press, 2001), 77, 82, 227–28.

34. Patricia Kugler, interview by author, January 22, 2010, written notes, p.1.

35. Otto's wife Daisy declared this directly to the author as a child, but it is probably impossible to verify. The Klan was prominent in central Nebraska towns near Lexington like North Platte, Curtis, and Grand Island; see Michael W. Schuyler, "The Ku Klux Klan in Nebraska, 1920–1930," *Nebraska History* 66 (1985): 234–56. Lexington had a Klan chapter; Russ Czaplewski, *Plum Creek to Lexington 1866–1939* (Lexington: Dawson County Historical Society, 1989), 95.

36. *Yellow Pages*, Lexington, Nebraska [telephone directories], 1932–50, Nebraska State Historical Society and the Dawson County Historical Museum. These directories provide four different addresses for Otto Kugler. He was listed at 1308 N. Madison St. in 1939 and 1940, and not listed after Marie's death in 1941 until 1948.

37. Interview with Patricia Kugler. On October 21, 1937, the *Clipper*'s "Ink Spots!" reported "'Ot' Kugler, operator on the Clipper force, has been confined to his home all week on account of sickness. He was stricken last Sunday and taken to the hospital where an examination disclosed that he may have to submit to a surgical operation in order to get relief. We know just how you feel 'Dutch' and you have our sympathy—but stay right in there and pitch." This would have occurred when Jimmy was five years old.

38. Marilyn Larson and Bonnie Tuma interviews by the author, July 31, 2010; Patricia Kugler, interview by the author. The twentieth century brought rural midwestern women new opportunities for employment outside the home and greater

independence; Thomas J. Morain, *Prairie Grass Roots: An Iowa Small Town in the Early Twentieth Century* (Ames: Iowa State University Press, 1988), 104.

39. I have not turned up the divorce in any county records. Jimmy remembered living alone with his grandmother and sitting at the kitchen table drawing long into the night. Reviewing Jimmy's school report cards, "Mrs. Otto Kugler" signed them each year until 1945/6, his eighth-grade year. "Otto Kugler" signed them in a distinctively different hand beginning in Jimmy's sophomore year. His report cards are in my possession.

40. In Jimmy's report card envelope is a cutting from the *Clipper* May 21, 1942, reporting his doing well in the Master Achievement test in reading and a class spelling test.

41. For examples from the *Clipper* (repeated in the *Dawson County Herald*), see March 21, April 25, and November 14, 1940; February 13, October 16, and December 4, 1941; January 14 and February 4, 1943; October 21, 1943; and April 27, 1944. I still have some of these collections of rattlesnake teeth and rattles, ocean coral, small rodent skulls, etc. that he carefully arranged in small boxes with identifying tags.

42. George Roeder, *The Censored War: American Visual Experience during World War Two* (New Haven: Yale University Press, 1993), 83.

43. For a sensitive and thoughtful account of censorship during the war, see Roeder, *The Censored War.*

44. Roeder, *The Censored War*, 11–14.

45. Roeder, *The Censored War*, 14–15, 19, 87, 92–93.

46. The *Clipper* discussed geography courses: February 26, 1941, December 9, 1943, January 6, 1944, February 24, 1944, and November 16, 1944; Jimmy's participation in patriotic fundraising is mentioned in issues from December 17, 1942, February 18, 1943 and March 25, 1943.

47. In the 1940s, the *Dawson County Herald* ran propagandistic versions of *Popeye*, *Steve Canyon*, etc. in support of the war effort. Whitman Publishing premiered the Big Little Books in 1932 and eventually published *Alley Oop*, *Mickey Mouse*, and *Dick Tracy*. Soon, other publishers like Dell and Fawcett also took them up. I remember these among my father's personal collection, especially one *Alley Oop* storyline from 1941 on travel to Egypt and the conflict over the magic belt, as well as later travel to the age of pirates. For the background and art of V. T. Hamlin, see R. C. Harvey, "A Stretch in the Bone Age: The Life and Cartooning Genius of V. T. Hamlin," *Comics Journal*, May 21, 2012, http://www.tcj.com/a-stretch-in-the-bone-age-the-life-and-cartooning-genius-of-v-t-hamlin/; Michael H. Price, "V. T. Hamlin and the Road to Moo," in V. T. Hamlin, *Alley Oop: 1939*, vol. 4 of *The Library of American Comics Essentials* (San Diego: IDW Publishing, 2013); Paul Tumey, "The

Precisely Rendered Blam: Alley Oop in 1939," *Comics Journal*, September 10, 2014, http://www.tcj.com/the-precisely-rendered-blam-alley-oop-in-1939/.

48. Howard P. Chudacoff, *Children at Play: An American History* (New York: New York University Press, 2007), 98–99, 116–18; Kriste Lindenmeyer, *The Greatest Generation Grows Up: American Childhood in the 1930s* (Chicago: Dee, 2005), 156–57; Gary Gross, *Kid's Stuff: Toys and the Changing World of American Childhood* (Cambridge, MA: Harvard University Press, 1997), 89–91.

49. See Gross, *Kid's Stuff*. My father would imitate The Whistler's distinctive tune, or intone in a sinister way the introduction—"Who knows what evil lurks in the hears of men? The Shadow knows!"—from that popular program. For the detective and Western dramas of the radio era, see J. Fred MacDonald, *Don't Touch That Dial: Radio Programming in American Life, 1920–1960* (Chicago: Nelson-Hall, 1982) According to the *Clipper*, the comics were read aloud over the local radio each Sunday from noon to 12:30; November 11, 1937.

50. E. Albert Moffett, "Hometown Radio in 1942: The Role of Local Stations during the First Year of Total War," *American Journalism* 3, no. 2 (1986): 87–98.

51. On these themes in the nationally broadcast "This Is War!" radio series, see James Spiller, "This Is War! Network Radio and World War II Propaganda in America," *Journal of Radio Studies* 11, no. 1 (2004): 55–72.

52. Jimmy was apparently friends with the theater owner's son and cleaned the lobby and did other odd jobs in exchange for passes; interview with Patricia Kugler.

53. *Clipper*, February 6, 1941; November 27, 1941. A string of war films, serious and comedic, followed through 1944: "Tanks a Million," "Blondie for Victory," "Flying Tigers," "Manila Calling," "Thunderbirds," "Star Spangled Rhythm," "Orphan of the Blitz," "Chetniks! The Fighting Guerrillas," "Hitler's Children" ("We Know What to Do to Women Who Are Not Fit to be Nazi Mothers!")," Yankee Doodle Dandy," "Crash Dive," "Desert Victory" ("The Rout of Rommel"), "Desperate Journey" (about Errol Flynn and a five-man commando raid to Berlin), and "Flying Fortress." For comedic films that may have helped move public opinion toward intervention before Pearl Harbor, see Don B. Morlan, "Slapstick Contributions to WWII Propaganda: The Three Stooges and Abbott and Costello," *Studies in Popular Culture* 17, no. 1 (October 1994): 29–43.

54. This RKO picture was a sequel of sorts to the earlier "Hitler's Children." On this film's character as vicious propaganda, see Thomas Doherty, *Projections of War: Hollywood, American Culture and World War II* (New York: Columbia University Press, 1993), 31–34, 137. There is a range of research on films of the World War II era. I've consulted Jeanine Basinger, *The World War II Combat Film: Anatomy of a Genre* (Middleton, CT: Wesleyan University Press, 2003); Lewis Jacobs, "World War II and the American Film," *Cinema Journal* 7 (Winter 1967–68): 1–21; Thomas Schatz, "World War II and the Hollywood 'War Film,'" in *Refiguring American Film Genres*, ed. Nick Browne

(Berkeley: University of California Press, 1998), 89–128; Peter C. Rollins, "World War II: Documentaries," and Robert Fyne, "World War II: Feature Films" in *The Columbia Companion to American History on Film: How the Movies Have Portrayed the American Past*, ed. Peter C. Rollins (New York: Columbia University Press, 2006), 116–36.

55. Wright, *Comic Book Nation*, 56–60; Savage Jr., *Commies, Cowboys, and Jungle Queens*, 12–13.

56. *Clipper*, September 25, 1941. Before Pearl Harbor, war comic books were filled with military planes. See for example *Air Fighters Comics* #1 (November 1941).

57. William M. Tuttle Jr., *"Daddys Gone to War": The Second World War in the Lives of Americas Children* (New York and Oxford: Oxford University Press, 1993).

58. Kimble, *Mobilizing the Home Front: War Bonds and Domestic Propaganda* (College Station: Texas A&M University Press, 2006); on bond ads designed to recruit school children see 49–50.

59. Kimble, *Mobilizing the Home Front*, 140–44. For a detailed account of how bond ads depicting dead or dying soldiers gradually shaped public expectations for images of military sacrifice, even before the famous September 20, 1943 *Life* magazine photo of three dead Marines, see Kimble, "Spectral Soldiers: Domestic Propaganda, Visual Culture, and Images of Death on the World War II Home Front," *Rhetoric and Public Affairs* 19, no. 4 (Winter 2016): 535–70.

60. For a wide range of propaganda posters, see William L. Bird Jr. and Harry R. Rubenstein, *Design for Victory: World War II Posters on the American Home Front* (New York: Princeton Architectural Press, 1998), in particular, 7, 29, 32–33, 45–47, 73, 77, 81, 90–91.

61. I've counted on several scholars for this background: John W. Dower, *War without Mercy: Race and Power in the Pacific War* (New York: Pantheon, 1986) discussed editorial writing and cartoons among other sources; for film, Doherty, *Projections of War.* Tuttle makes the closer connection between mass entertainment and the imaginative lives of children; *"Daddy's Gone to War,"* throughout but especially chap. 9.

62. For some commentary on this incongruity, see Kimble, *Mobilizing the Home Front*, 88–89. A nearly duplicated portrait by Joe Doolin appeared on the cover of *Rangers Comics* #19 (October 1941), only depicting the bayoneting of a Japanese soldier while in the foreground lies a trussed-up woman in a revealing floral dress.

63. Brian Sutton-Smith describes the "solitude" of the modern child at play in *Toys as Culture* (New York: Gardner Press, 1986), 24–25.

64. Tuttle suggests that Americans were typically more concerned about the war in the Pacific than in Europe. *"Daddy's Gone to War,"* 138. Germany had not attacked the US mainland though the Atlantic submarine war was grim and widely covered in the news. It is not hard to understand Americans on the West Coast being more concerned with the war in the Pacific.

65. A young Marine, Eugene Sledge, recalled the horrors years later; *With the Old Breed: At Peleliu and Okinawa* (Oxford: Oxford University Press, 1990). For a brief but moving summary see Paul Fussell, *The Boys' Crusade: The American Infantry in Northwestern Europe, 1944–1945* (New York: Modern Library, 2005).

66. Gross, *Kid's Stuff*, 103, 112–13; for the anarchistic quality of animated cartoons see 105.

67. Amato, *Re-Thinking Home*, 91–92, describes domestic anger in rural America and media representations as a legitimate outlet of violence. During the war, a wide range of violent portraits of Hitler and his Nazi princes, the German soldier, and Tojo, Hirohito, and the Japanese forces could be found in everything from the sale of breakfast cereal to postcards, toys, and board games. For some examples, see the anti-Axis and anti-Japanese items produced during the war: https://www.historyonthenet.com/authentichistory/1939-1945/2-homefront/.

68. Roeder, *The Censored War*, 82.

69. Milton Caniff, *The Complete Terry and the Pirates 1943–1944*, vol. 5 (San Diego: Library of American Comics, IDW Publishing, 2008), ed. Dean Mullaney and introductions by Russ Maheras and Bruce Canwell.

70. See "The Bald Eagle" in *Air Fighters Comics*, Hillman Productions #2 (November 1942), art by Harry Sahl.

71. "Airboy," *Air Fighters Comics* #9 (June 1943); the cover of *Captain Midnight* #21 (June 1944). For those stereotypes generally in comics, see Wright, *Comic Book Nation*, 45–47.

72. "Sky Wolf," *Air Fighters Comics* #5 (February 1943). An earlier episode of "Sky Wolf," *Air Fighters Comics* #2 (November 1942), drawn by Mort Leav and story by Harry Stein, tells of "Goro, the Tokyo Torturer," a huge, drooling Japanese hulk with fangs. Trained in Japan, he explains that he uses simpler torture devices only on those younger than two. His favorite is a chopper that takes three hours to saw off a man's head, which Hitler is excited to watch. For other examples see "Double Trouble in Tokyo," *Captain Midnight* #5 (February 1943). "The Beasts That Flew Like Birds" has Midnight battling giant vampire bats who attack bomber pilots. They are later revealed as disguised Japanese soldiers flying gliders.

73. "Sky Wolf," *Air Fighters Comics* #2 (November 1942); "Double Trouble in Tokyo," *Captain Midnight* #5 (February 1943). *Air Fighters*' cover of #9 (June 1943) edition depicts Airboy melting a tall, green, slant-eyed monster with a flamethrower.

74. On the artist's aspiration to feel true-life events in the act of creating their own narrations, see Richard Slotkin, "Fiction for the Purposes of History," *Rethinking History* 9, no. 2/3 (June/September 2005): 221–36; Sarah Pinto, "Emotional Histories and Historical Emotions: Looking at the Past in Historical Novels," *Rethinking History* 14, no. 2 (June 2010): 201.

75. Telephone interview with Nola (Jones) Reed. Reed implied that Jimmy and Kutz drew the comics with "the boys" in mind.

76. Fredric Wertham, *Seduction of the Innocent* (New York and Toronto: Rinehart and Co., 1954; 2nd ed,) 386.

77. Ginzburg explained the individual's interaction with provocative ideas and images in mass-produced form as a "filter;" *The Cheese and the Worms*, xi–xii, xv. Ginzburg concentrated on recovering a pre-literate culture trapped in official documents. Of course, children also have an oral culture difficult to recapture. I have no access to any such sources through Jimmy's comics.

78. Gerald Linderman, *Embattled Courage: The Experience of Combat in the American Civil War* (New York: Free Press, 1989), 1.

79. On the creative diversity of comic perspective, see Scott McCloud, *Understanding Comics* (New York: Harper Paperbacks, 1994).

80. Tuttle, *"Daddys Gone to War,"* 5–12; R. Douglas Hurt, *The Great Plains during World War II* (Lincoln: University of Nebraska Press, 2008), 28, 31, 88–91; Robert B. Westbrook, "Fighting for the American Family: Private Interests and Political Obligation in World War II," in *The Power of Culture: Critical Essays in American History*, ed. Richard Wrightman Fox, T. J. Jackson Lears, and Robert B. Westbrook (Chicago: University of Chicago, 1993), 195–221. For examples from propaganda and bond posters, see Bird and Rubenstein, *Design for Victory*, 29, 90–91.

81. *Zip Comics* #22 (January 1944), cover by Irv Novick; *Liberty Scouts* #2 (June 1941), cover by Paul Guvstavson; *Pep Comics* #4 (May 1940), cover by Irv Novick; *Fight Comics* #15 (October 1941), cover by Dan Zolnerowich; *Wings Comics* #37 (September 1943), cover by Art Saaf. Alex Shomburg's cover for *Exciting Comics* #39 (June 1945) showed Nazi soldiers making poisonous candy while through a window other soldiers give it out to ragged children in a ruined America. A range of covers depicted children threatened by Nazis or Japanese monsters.

82. John Judy and Brad Palmer, "Boys on the Battlefield: Kid-Combatants as Propaganda in World War II-Era Comic Books;" John R. Katsion, "The *Boy Commandos* Comic Book as Equipment for Living: The Comic Book Form as Propaganda," both in Goodnow and Kimble, eds., *The 10 Cent War*, 67, 81–82, respectively.

83. Roeder, *The Censored War*, 59–61.

84. On this stereotype promoted in both American and Japanese propaganda, see Dower, *War without Mercy.*

85. Flogging and torture stood out in *Hitler's Children* (1942) and *Behind the Rising Sun* (1943); Doherty, *Projections of War*, 53–54. *The Purple Heart* (1944) was the first American film to depict the Japanese torture of POWs; ibid, 50–51. Dower discusses Japanese and German torture in American propaganda in *War without Mercy*, chap. 3, especially 46–52 and 129.

86. Since "The Battle of Toadajima" clearly echoes the American battle on Iwo Jima of February 19–March 26, 1945—when Jimmy was thirteen—he had to have drawn this portion of his saga following reports of that bloody battle.

87. The church he depicts with the distinctive tall steeple seems to resemble most closely the town's Catholic Church caught in a 1909 postcard highlighting Lexington buildings, including the distinctive bank: https://www.hippostcard.com/listing/lexington-nebraskarr-depotchurcheshigh-schoolbank1909-real-photorppc/34160134. The Novelty Press stories highlighted realistic young characters from small towns, whose idealism, integrity, and decency idealized the fight for American liberty; see David E. Wilt, "'Everyone Can Help, Young or Old, Large or Small': Novelty Press Mobilizes Its Readers," in Goodnow and Kimble, eds., *The 10 Cent War*, 88–90. However, as I'll show, Jimmy's characters exhibited little or none of such idealized virtues other than outrage and vengeance.

88. In one scene from "The Fall of Frogington," a piece of Frog field artillery has the spoked wheels of Great War artillery, perhaps because such a machine is more interesting and distinctive. But one artillery piece, the 105 mm M2 howitzer, dated from the early 1930s and had spoked wheels.

89. For the possible colonial, even racist, undertones of jungle settings, see Wright, *Comic Book Nation*, 31.

90. For "lost cause" and "last stand" battles as a critical part of the combat movie genre, see Basinger, *The World War II Combat Film*, chap.1.

91. For the equally disastrous defeats in the Asian Pacific of the British and Dutch, see John Keegan, *The Second World War* (New York: Penguin Books, 1989), chap. 13

92. Gene Fawcette, who worked in the Eisner & Iger shop, seems to have made this a specialty, with dramatic and beautifully crafted scenes in #3 (November 1940), #10 (June 1941), and #20 (April 1942).

93. This re-creates a pivotal scene from an early aerial combat film *Flying Tigers* (1942) starring John Wayne. The Majestic showed this film in November of 1942; *Clipper*, November 12, 1942. Such an incident also occurred in the films *Wake Island* (1942) and *Air Force* (1943), but they were not advertised in the *Clipper* or the *Herald* so it is unknown if they played in Lexington. L. B. Cole's cover for the September issue of *Contact Comics* (1944) depicted descending US paratroopers shooting Japanese fighter pilots. Shooting defenseless soldiers did occur, committed also by US troops; Adams, *The Best War Ever*, 110.

94. Several articles in popular mainstream magazines reported their remarkable accomplishments. Russell Whelan's bestselling account, *The Flying Tigers*, appeared the next year, followed by Tiger pilot Col. Robert L. Scott's memoir, *God Is My Co-Pilot*.

95. In "The Fate of a Toad Convoy," Jimmy kept a running tally of ships and planes destroyed, perhaps an echo of the concluding count of destroyed Japanese ships and planes in John Ford's 1942 documentary *The Battle of Midway*. The seminal combat film *Bataan* (1943), where a squad courageously fights superior numbers of cruel Japanese soldiers until the last, played at the Majestic in September 1943; *Clipper*, September 30, 1943. For an analysis of such films and their context, see Basinger, *The World War II Combat Film*, 34, 58–63.

96. The best introduction to these elements of the World War II combat film remains Basinger, *The World War II Combat Film*, chap. 1.

97. On this, see Richard Overy, *The Bombing War: Europe, 1939–1945* (New York: Penguin, 2013). For a brisk discussion of some Allied commitment to terror bombing, as well its service to vengeance for the Blitz and Pearl Harbor, see Charles S. Maier, "Targeting the City: Debates and Silences about the Aerial Bombing of World War II," *International Review of the Red Cross* 87, no. 859 (September 2005): 429–44.

98. The flamethrower seemed perfectly suited to a cinematic report of war, but the soldiers assigned it often hated its grisly results and were specially targeted by opposing troops; Adams, *The Best War Ever*, 74.

99. Stephen McCreery and Brian Creech, "The Journalistic Value of Emerging Technologies: American Press Reaction to Newsreels during World War II," *Journalism History* 40, no. 3 (Fall 2014): 177–86.

100. Doherty, *Projections of War*, 136, 244–50.

101. This documentary of the last phases of the battle of Peleliu (September 15, 1944 to November 27, 1944) showed, among other things, jungle patrols, beach landings, and fire exchanges at close quarters. *With the Marines at Tarawa* depicted a Japanese soldier torn to bits by machine gun fire, though censored from most civilian prints.

102. For the persistent theme of war-era comic books that fighting was the masculine norm, even an adventurous, fun means of killing a morally depraved enemy, see Judy and Palmer, "Boys on the Battlefield," 69–76.

103. Karasik, *Turn Loose Our Death Rays and Kill Them All!*; Chester Gould, *The Complete Dick Tracy: Dailies & Sundays*, vol. 8 (San Diego: IDW Press, 2009), September 13–15, 1943.

104. For a comic book example of the kinds of brutal hand-to-hand combat possible in portraits of the Pacific theater, see *War Heroes* #9 (July/September 1944).

105. The movie earned big ad space in the *Lexington Clipper*: December 2 and 9, 1943. For evidence of the growth of and widespread popular fascination with US airpower, see Steve Call, "Here's Your Air War: Popular Culture Depictions of Land-Based Air Power in the Pacific," in *War in the American Pacific and East Asia, 1941–1972*,

ed. Hal M. Friedman (Lexington: University Press of Kentucky, 2018), 54–92; on Severtsky's *Victory*, see 78–81.

106. For defenses of civilian "area bombing" by contemporaries, see former British Principal Secretary of the Air Ministry J. M. Spaight, *Bombing Vindicated* (London: G. Bless, 1944); Haywood S. Hansell Jr., Major General, USAF (ret.), *The Strategic Air War against Germany and Japan: A Memoir* (Washington, DC: Office of Air Force History, 1986), who commanded bomber groups in the European and Pacific theaters. The US official postwar surveys of aerial bombing for Europe and the Pacific reached similar conclusions. For the history of area or strategic bombing, I've consulted: Christopher C. Harmon, "'Are We Beasts?': Churchill and the Moral Question of World War II 'Area Bombing,'" *The Newport Papers* #1 (Center for Naval Warfare Studies, December 1991); Thomas Childers, "Facilis descensus averni est: The Allied Bombing of Germany and the Issue of German Suffering." *Central European History* 38, no. 1 (2008): 75–105; Overy, *The Bombing War*; and Conrad C. Crane, *American Airpower Strategy in World War II: Bombs, Cities, Civilians, and Oil* (Lawrence: University Press of Kansas, 2016).

107. Hamlin offered a fun solution to this in his January 7, 1941 strip; see *Alley Oop: 1939*, 16.

108. Jordan Braverman argues that the press and middlebrow authors were far more sympathetic in their depictions of German civilians than of the Japanese; *To Hasten the Homecoming: How Americans Fought World War II through the Media* (1996; Lanham, MD: Rowman and Littlefield, 2015), 192–94.

109. Jimmy's drawing of sinister eyes and sharply defined teeth may vaguely reflect racist depictions of the slanted eyes and prominent teeth—in some cases fangs—of propaganda portraits of the Japanese. As the figure suggests, sinister eyes and fanged teeth represented evil Frogs no less than the Toads. In some later comics, Jimmy depicted three distinct battle royal fights between "Black Frogs" with the distinctive shark teeth and sinister eyes and "White Frogs." Sometimes the darker Frogs are hairy. But his intentions, other than creating distinctions for the combatants, is not clear. For racist images in toys and children's goods in this period, see Gross, *Kid's Play*, 97–98. For an excellent and very readable model of interpreting comics with an eye to race discourse, though outside the bounds of this study, see Qiana Whitted, *EC Comics: Race, Shock, and Social Protest* (New Brunswick: Rutgers University Press, 2019).

110. Jarvis describes the ideal white, youthful, muscular males of the WWII era and national goals for restored attention to physical education, sports, and psychological health in serving combat readiness. But Jimmy's Frogs suggest little of this. Only the Toads, in their semi-monstrous villainy, may recall propagandist and racist depictions of the Japanese; *The Male Body at War*, 138–39.

111. John Harry "Jack" Kutz died in 2006; his wife LeDonna (also from Lexington) died a few years earlier. For Kutz's obituary, see: http://obits.abqjournal.com/obits/2006/12/13.

112. Myrl Sage, interview by author.

113. Marilyn Larsen, interview by author. The *Clipper* October 21, 1943 reported that Jack Kutz had drawn several different kinds of ships for the class unit on maritime history. Mrs. Larsen could not remember Jimmy as an artist or much of a student, for that matter.

114. For example, the *Clipper* December 14, 1939, March 21, 1940 (second grade) and November 14, 1940 (third grade). These kinds of reports grow more frequent in the fourth grade: October 16 and 30, December 4, 1941, January 8 and April 30, 1942. Jimmy is frequently mentioned in such articles for the fifth grade but not for drawing. The next year (October 21, 1943), his friend Jack Kutz received recognition for drawing historical ships for a classroom unit. Jimmy was recognized later (April 27, 1944) for drawings of Africa.

115. *Clipper*, February 14, 1946 in "Junior High Notes" reported that "the seventh grade art classes have on display some very good likenesses of comic strip characters which they have drawn." Jimmy and Jack Kutz were in the eighth grade that year, but it is possible that they did such work the year before. For the use of cartoons in the American classroom curriculum, see Carol L. Tilley, "Educating with Comics," in *The Secret Origins of Comics Studies*, ed. Mathew J. Smith and Randy Duncan (New York and Abingdon: Routledge, 2017), 3–11.

116. Interview with Nola (Jones) Reed.

117. For the first grade, the *Clipper* (March 23, 1939) reported, "We think Jimmie [sic] Kugler must treasure that mouse he brought to school Thursday morning." In the second grade, Jimmy reportedly observed birds for class and made charts of them; February 22 and March 14, 1940. In the fourth-grade hobby show, Jimmy brought his scrapbooks, "one of animal pictures, the other of airplanes," September 25, 1941.

118. Jimmy kept these books with his comic strip collection, some comic books and Big Little Books, his report cards, and his high school diploma.

119. See for example Charles Lederer, *The Junior Cartoonist—Presenting a Simple Course in Drawing, Painting and Caricature—Combining Amusement and Instruction* (Chicago: Monarch Book Company, 1906), no page numbers; for the folk singer Frog, see E. C. Matthews, *How to Draw Funny Pictures: A Complete Guide to Cartooning, with 200 illustrations by Zim*, 2nd ed. (1928; Chicago: Frederick Drake, 1944), 75.

120. As intelligent, bipedal amphibians, Jimmy's Frogs remind me of the humanoid Newts in Czech novelist Karel Čapek's remarkable 1936 dystopian and anti-colonial fantasy, *War with the Newts*. Though translated into English within a year of publication, I have a hard time imagining Jimmy finding a copy in Lexington.

121. For some examples of wartime comic book covers, see "Deconstructing Propaganda: World War II Comic Book Covers—Images of the Enemy: Episode 9, Japan," https://www.youtube.com/watch?v=tId_EcrkDOQ.

122. In *Maus*, chap. 2, "Time Flies," and several other places, Art Spiegelman depicted his characters as humans wearing animal masks; *The Complete Maus* (New York: Pantheon Books, 1996).

123. There is one plump Frog in Jimmy's later comics wielding a machine gun against a dozen more typically thin Frogs.

124. Smith's death in 1935 saw Gus Edson take on the strip. One *Gumps* cartoon, promoting war bonds, appeared in the *Dawson County Herald*, June 18, 1942. I thank Randy Jackson of Michigan State University's Special Collections for leading me to Edson's work.

125. Disney took a significant role in marketing and shaping American childhood imagination; Chudacoff, *Children at Play*, 124–25. In the 1930s, comic books and so-called fantasy toys were closely connected; Gross, *Kid's Stuff*, 100–102.

126. Ub Iwerks created Mickey Mouse; he developed Flip for his own studio during a hiatus from working for Disney. The *Clipper* for October 28, 1937 under "Notes of Interest in Lexington High School" announced that along with a film about Holland, "Disney's 'Flippety the Frog'" would be shown in the school auditorium. Flip the Frog can still be seen in the DVD collections *Cartoons That Time Forgot: The Ub Iwerks Collection* (Image Entertainment, 1993), vols. 1 and 2.

127. *The Soldiers' Tale: Bearing Witness to a Modern War* (New York: Viking, 1997), 19.

128. From the beginning of the war, journalists cooperated with military leaders to create the myth of "the good war" for the American public; see Adams, *The Best War Ever*, chap. 1.

129. Basinger, *The World War II Combat Film*, 67–69; on the role of women in the classic Western, see Richard Slotkin, *Gunfighter Nation: The Myth of the Frontier in Twentieth-Century America* (New York: Atheneum, 1992), chaps. 10 and 11.

130. For some background on popular and propagandistic depictions of masculinity before and during the war, see Martha Banta, *Barbaric Intercourse: Caricature and the Culture of Conduct, 1841–1936* (Chicago: University of Chicago Press, 2003), 323–25; and Jarvis, *The Male Body at War*.

131. Lepore, *The Secret History of Wonder Woman*, 196–201. Marston conceived the character to be both the equal of and a gender contrast to Superman, Batman, and Captain America. But Wonder Woman's pin-up, badass feminism did not survive the postwar change in comic taste, nor in the early 1950s, Wertham's attacks, the Senate Subcommittee hearings on juvenile delinquency, and the resulting Comics Code; Lepore, 238–39, 271–72.

132. "The Changing Face of Children's Culture," in *Reinventing Childhood after World War II*, ed. Paula S. Fass and Michael Grossberg (Philadelphia: University of Pennsylvania Press, 2011), 39.

133. *Juvenile Delinquency (Comic Books): Hearings Before the Subcommittee to Investigate Juvenile Delinquency of the Committee on the Judiciary United States Senate. Eighty-Third Congress, Second Session Pursuant to S. 190 Investigation of Juvenile Delinquency in the United States. April 21, 22, and June 4, 1954* (printed for the use of the Committee on the Judiciary; United States Government Printing Office, 1954), 154–55. On Bender, see Lepore, *The Secret History of Wonder Woman*, 207–8.

134. For a reflection on the roots of comic book art and drama in the anxious lives of largely Jewish artists in the urban East, see Jones, *Men of Tomorrow*, 128, 232–33. Throughout, Jones vividly describes the drive, anger, and resentment expressed by these young male artists in their dynamic superhero, horror, and true crime comics of the later 1940s and early 1950s.

135. Fass, *The End of American Childhood*, does not appear to give much attention to the childhoods of the small American towns of the 1920s through the 1940s. In the wake of the new "scientific" approach to childrearing and education, what of the kid who did not see school as the new and attractive defining force in their life? As an opportunity to escape from home?

136. Wright, *Comic Book Nation*, 142, 147.

137. *Clipper*, August 27, 1942.

138. By the early twentieth century, modern media encouraged rural idealizations of country life contrasted to stereotypes of the city: Don S. Kirschner, *City and Country: Rural Responses to Urbanization in the 1920s* (Westport, CT: Greenwood, 1970), 57–58, 249. For the greater regulation of classroom patriotism in the US as well as personal hygiene and health, see Lindenmeyer, *The Greatest Generation Grows Up*, 119–20. Tuttle described how the war ratcheted up such progressive programs to teach patriotic virtues like cooperation and self-sacrifice for the sake of order and victory; *"Daddy's Gone to War,"* chap. 7, particularly 127, 132–33.

139. *Strange Suspense: The Steve Ditko Archives*, ed. Blake Bell (Seattle: Fantagraphic Books, 2009), vols. 1, 9. See also Andrew Hultkrans, "Steve Ditko's Hands," in *Give Our Regards to the Atomsmashers! Writers on Comics*, ed. Geoff Dyer (New York: Pantheon Books, 2004), 218, 224.

140. For this definition, see Philip J. Nickel, "Horror and the Idea of Everyday Life: On Skeptical Threats in *Psycho* and *The Birds*," in Thomas Fahey, ed., *The Philosophy of Horror* (Lexington: University of Kentucky Press, 2012), 14–15. The notion of "art horror" and its relationship to narrations of danger, dread, and disgust are found in Noël Carroll, *The Philosophy of Horror: Or, Paradoxes of the Heart* (New York: Routledge, 1990), chap.1.

141. In Olav Christensen's study of Norwegian snowboarders, kids imitate tricks they see in documentaries and magazines. By doing so, they aspire to membership in the snowboarding community and re-create the tricks in their own fashion. The snowboarding world of great riders raises the ceiling of possibility and becomes their world, the world in which they imagine themselves as full members; "Board with the World: Youthful Approaches to Landscapes and Mediascapes," in *Designing Modern Childhoods: History, Space, and the Material Culture of Children*, ed. Marta Gutman and Ning de Coninck-Smith (New Brunswick: Rutgers University Press, 2008), 282–300.

142. Adams, *The Best War Ever*.

143. Adams, *The Best War Ever*, 102. For examples and sources of the shocking, macabre nature of warfare in World War II, see especially chaps. 4 and 5.

144. Hillary Chute argues for the "feminized" character of comics, not only in their "mass" or "low" character, but more importantly on how each frame presents the comic's dependence on the "space" of the image conjoined to "time." She emphasizes this quality in contrast to the more "masculine" character of words read, expressed, and heard; *Graphic Women: Life Narrative and Contemporary Comics* (New York: Columbia University Press, 2010), 10. At most, this can suggest that the comic form in no technical way resists women telling their authentic, intimate stories. But in Jimmy's case the comic form let him participate intimately in the past, creatively retold in ways typically masculine and violent. Alison Mandaville argues that Megan Kelso's revising of the American Founding era, especially of Hamilton and his relationships, is a self-consciously feminist and democratic history of America. The comics are her perspective on the past, in which creating a history-inspired comic story lets her participate intimately "back then." "'Duel. I'll Give You a DUEL': Intimacy and History in Megan Kelso's *Alexander Hamilton Trilogy*," in Pustz, *Comic Books and American Cultural History*, 59–75.

145. For comics as fundamentally anarchistic and outrageous, see Bradford Wright, "Comic books," *The Encyclopedia of Popular Culture* (Detroit: St. James Press, 2000), vol 1, 560. On the decline by domestication of superhero comic book violence after the war, see Wright, *Comic Book Nation*, 57–60. This contrasts a good deal of the "underground" comic tradition in which anarchism serves philosophical and moral depth; Tabachnick, "Of *Maus* and Memory," 154.

146. Westbrook, "Fighting for the American Family."

147. Michael Lesy created a fascinating if provocative portrait of the terror and madness he suggested was occasionally beneath the surface of rural American life, against which the city represented a utopia of licensed adolescent escape; *Wisconsin Death Trip* (New York: Anchor Books, 1973, 1991). See also Amato, *Rethinking Home*, chap. 6.

148. On these elements in jungle settings for the combat movie, see Basinger, *The World War II Combat Film*, 124–26.

149. For a brief outline of the jungle comic genre see Savage, *Commies, Cowboys, and Jungle Queens*, 76–79.

150. Jones, *Men of Tomorrow*, 143, 153. See also Scott Bukatman, *Matters of Gravity: Special Effects and Supermen in the 20th Century* (Durham: Duke University Press, 2003).

151. For the reader's fabrication and recrafting of mass media and government information into her own stories, especially reworking the experience of the city at the "street" level, see Michel de Certeau, *The Practice of Everyday Life*, trans. Steven Rendall (Berkeley: University of California Press, 1984), especially chap. 7.

152. Savage, *Commies, Cowboys, and Jungle Queens*, 12, 116–17; Wright, *Comic Book Nation*, 75–84, and chap. 4; Hajdu, *The Ten-Cent Plague*, 39–43, 60–69, 92–94; Carol L. Tilley, "Seducing the Innocent: Fredric Wertham and the Falsifications That Helped Condemn Comics," *Information & Culture: A Journal of History* 47, no. 4 (2012): 383–413.

153. "Famous Tales of Terror: The Black Cat," *Yellowjacket Comics* #1 (1944), art by Bill Allison; at http://professorhswaybackmachine.blogspot.com/2018/05/poe-1944-pt-5.html. See Lawrence Watt-Evans, "The Other Guys," originally in *The Scream Factory* #19 (1997), reproduced at http://www.watt-evans.com/theotherguys.shtml.

154. Doherty, *Projections of War*, 272–73; Basinger, *The World War II Combat Film*, 161–67.

155. For examples of such images in combat comics of World War II, see the flame-thrower on *The United States Marines* #3 (1943), cover by Creig Flessel; bayonetting on *Rangers Comics* #19 (October 1941), Joe Doolin cover; a Japanese pilot bleeding from the mouth on *Air Fighters Comics* #2 (November 1942), Charles Biro cover, and a beheading on *Fight Comics* #31 (April 1944), cover by Joe Doolin. Depictions of Nazis as monsters or commanding monsters are too numerous to count; for a few examples see *U.S.A. Comics* #14 (1944), Sol Brodsky cover, *Pep Comics* #34 (December 1942), cover by Bob Fujitani, *Mystic Comics* #8 (March 1942), cover by Al Gabrielle.

156. "Americans pulled a lid of tense harmony down on themselves, while a stew of fear and disgust bubbled under it." Hajdu, *The Ten-Cent Plague*, 231–35.

157. Savage, *Commies, Cowboys, and Jungle Queens*, 15–17, 115–17.

158. Wright, *Comic Book Nation*, 75, 77, 83–84. Jones's insightful *Men of Tomorrow*, 232–34, 353, extends these claims largely from Savage and Wright.

Conclusion

1. "Newfoundland Novelist Michael Crummey on the 'Appalling Confusion" of Childhood,'" *The Sunday Magazine*, CBC radio, August 16, 2019, at https://www.cbc.ca/radio/sunday/the-sunday-edition-for-august-18-2019-1.5248831/newfoundland-novelist-michael-crummey-on-the-appalling-confusion-of-childhood-1.5248849.

2. On counter-factual historical narratives in novels, especially those about World War II as driven by creating a more interesting or hopeful outcome than what really happened, see Richard J. Evans, *Altered Pasts: Counterfactuals in History* (Boston: Little, Brown Book Group, 2014).

3. On this, see *Historical Reenactment: From Realism to the Affective Turn*, ed. Iain McCalman and Paula A. Pickering (Basingstroke and New York: Palgrave Macmillan, 2010).

4. For a depiction of some of the concerns about American moral character, masculinity, and civic health before the war, see Jarvis, *The Male Body at War*, chap. 1. A quite different portrait of Depression-era youth as idealistic activists can be found in Britt Haas, *Fighting Authoritarianism: American Youth Activism in the 1930s* (New York: Fordham University Press, 2017).

5. In this way, Jimmy's comics sharply contrast Savage's description of mainstream comics following Pearl Harbor: "War concerned all Americans, and the cooperation of all would be required to insure [sic] a successful conclusion. It was not, as a rule, a time for cultural fun." *Commies, Cowboys, and Jungle Queens*, 9; also 11–12.

6. For a representative selection of the Timely/Atlas war comics of the 1950s, see *Marvel Masterworks: Atlas Era Battlefield*, ed. Hank Chapman, Don Rico, and Michael J. Vassallo (New York: Marvel Worldwide, 2011), vol. 1; *Atlas at War! Russ Heath, Stan Lee, Gene Colan, Syd Shores, John Severin, Don Heck, Steve Ditko, Jack Kirby, and More*, ed. Michael J. Vassallo (New York: Dead Reckoning/Marvel, 2020).

7. On the unnaturalness of "art horror" erupting from the taken-for-granted world, see Noël Carroll, *The Philosophy of Horror*.

8. On the transition to comic book horror in the late 1940s and early 1950s, see Hajdu, *The Ten-Cent Plague*, chaps. 3 and 4; Wright, *Comic Book Nation*, chaps. 3 and 4. Basinger has commented on the relationship between horror film motifs and those of a combat film like *Bataan* in *The World War II Combat Film*, 61, 138–39.

9. For the loss of reader interest in superhero comics, see Wilt, "'Everyone Can Help, Young or Old, Large or Small,' in Goodnow and Kimble, eds., *The 10 Cent War*, 185–86.

10. Richard Reynolds, *Super Heroes: A Modern Mythology* (Jackson: University Press of Mississippi, 1992).

11. Cord, *Comics and Conflict*; Hajdu, *The Ten-Cent Plague*. Also, see Jones, *Men of Tomorrow*, 173, 225.

12. For Hanks, see Karasik, *Turn Loose Our Death Rays and Kill Them All!*

13. "Certificate of Church Membership," dated April 2, 1944, in my possession.

14. The ads in The *Lexington Clipper* on November 18, 1943 devoted a large space to visiting evangelist J. J. Williamson, Director, Bible Auditorium of the Air; "Is This War Armageddon?," "Don't Miss this Startling Presentation, Straight from the Bible on a Question Puzzling Millions." The week's program included: "World's Greatest

Criminal," "Who is he? Hitler or Hirohito?," "Four Mysterious Horsemen Riding Through the World," and "White, Red, Black and Pale. What do they mean?" A big ad on Dec. 2, 1943 promised Williamson would return to speak on "The United States in Prophecy." Also on November 23, 1943, the *Clipper* used another large ad to promote evangelist Lyman W. Shaw's talks on "God's Outline of Four World Empires," "A World Dictator for 1260 Years. The reign of the great anti-Christ," and "The Greatest Event in History Approaches." On January 6, 1944, the *Clipper* reported that Shaw would return to Lexington to speak on "Seven Terrible Plagues Coming," "Upon Whom Will They Fall?," "Have They Already Begun?" Finally, the March 30, 1944 paper promised Shaw would speak on "The Indispensable Man—Who Is He? Is He Roosevelt, Churchill, or Stalin?"

15. "Comics in a Man's Life," in *Give My Regards to the Atomsmashers!*, 39–41.

16. Carol L. Tilley, "Children and the Comics: Young Readers Take on the Critics," in *Protest on the Page: Essays on Print and the Culture of Dissent Since 1865*, ed. James L. Baughman, Jennifer Ratner-Rosenhagen, and James P. Danky (Madison: University of Wisconsin Press, 2015), 161–79. For contemporary defenses of comic books for children, see the essays in the special edition of the *Journal of Educational Sociology*, "The Comics as an Educational Medium," 18, no. 4 (December 1944); and Gladys Denny Schultz, "Comics, Radio, Movies: What Are They Doing to Our Children? And What Should Parents Do about Them?," *Better Homes and Gardens* 24 (November 1945): 22–23, 73–75.

17. Patricia Johnston argues that "low" or "popular" culture can suggest the resistance of a creative outsider or marginal person against an authority claiming to act in their best interests; "Introduction," in Patricia Johnston, ed., *Seeing High and Low: Representing Social Conflict in American Visual Culture* (Berkeley: University of California Press, 2006), 11.

18. "Childhood Studies and History: Catching a Culture in High Relief," in *The Children's Table: Childhood Studies and the Humanities*, ed. Anna Mae Duane (Athens: University of Georgia Press, 2013), 57.

Bibliography

Archival Sources

Dawson County Historical Society
The Minuteman. 1946–1950. Lexington High School Yearbook.
The Lexington Clipper. 1938–1950.
The Dawson County Herald. 1938–1950.
Yellow Pages. 1936–1950. Lexington, Nebraska.
Michigan State University Special Collections
Nebraska State Historical Society Library and Archives

Interviews

Kugler, Patricia. 2010. Interview by author. Portland, Oregon. January 22.
Larson, Marilyn. 2010. Interview by author. Lexington, NE. July 31.
Reed, Nola. 2021. Telephone interview by author. Orange City, IA. June 3.
Sage, Myrl. 2010. Telephone interview by author. Lexington, NE. July 30.
Tuma, Bonnie. 2010. Interview by author. Lexington, NE. July 31.

Secondary Sources

Adams, Michael C. C. *The Best War Ever: America and World War II*. Baltimore: Johns Hopkins University Press, 1994.
Amato, Joseph A. *Rethinking Home: A Case for Writing Local History*. Berkeley: University of California Press, 2002.

Banta, Martha. *Barbaric Intercourse: Caricature and the Culture of Conduct, 1841–1936*. Chicago: University of Chicago Press, 2003.

Basinger, Jeanine. *The World War II Combat Film: Anatomy of a Genre*. Middleton: Wesleyan University Press, 2003.

Beidler, Phillip D. *The Good War's Greatest Hits: World War II and American Remembering*. Atlanta: University of Georgia Press, 1998.

Bell, Blake, ed. *Strange Suspense: The Steve Ditko Archives*. Vol. 1. Seattle: Fantagraphic Books, 2009.

Betts, Raymond F., and Lyz Bly. *A History of Popular Culture: More of Everything, Faster and Brighter*, 2nd ed. London and New York: Routledge, 2013.

Bird, William L., Jr., and Harry R. Rubenstein. *Design for Victory: World War II Posters on the American Home Front*. New York: Princeton Architectural Press, 1998.

Braverman, Jordan. *To Hasten the Homecoming: How Americans Fought World War II through the Media*. 1996; Lanham, MD: Rowman and Littlefield, 2015.

Brooks, James F., Christopher R. N. DeCorse, and John Walton, eds. *Small Worlds: Method, Meaning and Narrative in Microhistory*. Santa Fe: School for Advanced Research Press, 2008.

Bukatman, Scott. *Matters of Gravity: Special Effects and Supermen in the 20th Century*. Durham: Duke University Press, 2003.

Call, Steve. "Here's Your Air War: Popular Culture Depictions of Land-Based Air Power in the Pacific." In *War in the American Pacific and East Asia, 1941–1972*, edited by Hal M. Friedman, 54–92. Lexington: University Press of Kentucky, 2018.

Caniff, Milton. *The Complete Terry and the Pirates 1943–1944*, edited by Dean Mullaney. Vol. 5. San Diego: Library of American Comics, IDW Publishing, 2008.

Carlton, Frank Tracy. *The History and Problems of Organized Labor*. Boston: D.C. Heath, 1911.

Carroll, Noël. *The Philosophy of Horror or Paradoxes of the Heart*. New York: Routledge, 1990.

Cartoons That Time Forgot: The Ub Iwerks Collection. Vols. 1 and 2. Image Entertainment, 1993.

Chambliss, Julian C., William L. Svitavsky, and Thomas C. Donaldson, eds. *Ages of Heroes, Eras of Men: Superheroes and the American Experience*. Newcastle upon Tyne: Cambridge Scholars Publishing, 2013.

Chapman, Hank, Don Rico, and Michael J. Vassallo, eds. *Marvel Masterworks: Atlas Era Battlefield*. Vol. 1. New York: Marvel Worldwide, 2011.

Childers, Thomas. "Facilis descensus averni est: The Allied Bombing of Germany and the Issue of German Suffering." *Central European History* 38, no. 1 (2008): 75–105.

Christensen, Olav. "Board with the World: Youthful Approaches to Landscapes and Mediascapes." In *Designing Modern Childhoods: History, Space, and the Material Culture of Children*, edited by Marta Gutman and Ning de Coninck-Smith, 282–300. New Brunswick: Rutgers University Press, 2008.

Chudacoff, Howard P. *Children at Play: An American History.* New York: New York University Press, 2007.

Chute, Hillary. "The Shadow of a Past Time: History and Graphic Representation in 'Maus.'" *Twentieth Century Literature* 52 no. 2 (Summer 2006): 199–230.

Chute, Hillary. *Graphic Women: Life Narrative and Contemporary Comics.* New York: Columbia University Press, 2010.

"The Comics as an Educational Medium" (theme edition), *Journal of Educational Sociology* 18, no. 4 (December 1944).

Cord, Scott. *Comics and Conflict: Patriotism and Propaganda from WWII through Operation Iraqi Freedom.* Annapolis: Naval Institute Press, 2014.

Crane, Conrad C. *American Airpower Strategy in World War II: Bombs, Cities, Civilians, and Oil.* Lawrence: University Press of Kansas, 2016.

Crummey, Michael. "The 'Appalling Confusion' of Childhood." *The Sunday Magazine*, CBC radio, August 16, 2019. https://www.cbc.ca/radio/sunday/the-sunday-edition-for-august-18-2019-1.5248831/newfoundland-novelist-michael-crummey-on-the-appalling-confusion-of-childhood-1.5248849.

Cullen, Jim. *The Art of Democracy: A Concise History of Popular Culture in the United States*, 2nd ed. New York: Monthly Review Press, 2002.

Czaplewski, Russ. *Plum Creek to Lexington, 1866–1939.* Lexington, NE: Dawson County Historical Society, 1989.

Davies, Richard O., Joseph A. Amato, and David R. Pichaske, eds. *A Place Called Home: Writings on the Midwestern Small Town.* St. Paul: Minnesota Historical Society Press, 2003.

De Certeau, Michel. *The Practice of Everyday Life.* Translated by Steven Rendall. Berkeley: University of California Press, 1984.

Doherty, Thomas. *Projections of War: Hollywood, American Culture, and World War II.* New York: Columbia University Press, 1993.

Dower, John W. *War without Mercy: Race and Power in the Pacific War.* New York: Pantheon, 1986.

Drozd, David, and Jerry Deichert. "Nebraska Historical Populations: Quick Reference Tables." University of Nebraska at Omaha: Center of Public Affairs Research, 2018. https://www.unomaha.edu/college-of-public-affairs-and-community-service/center-for-public-affairs-research/documents/nebraska-historical-population-report-2018.pdf.

Ellis, Mark. "Casualties of War: Buffalo County, Nebraska and Its World War II Dead," *Nebraska History* 101, no. 3 (Fall, 2020): 106–21.
Evans, Richard. *Altered Pasts: Counterfactuals in History*. Boston: Little, Brown Book Group, 2013.
Fass, Paula S. "Childhood and Memory," *Journal of the History of Childhood and Youth* 3, no. 2 (Spring 2010): 155–64.
Fass, Paula S. *The End of American Childhood: A History of Parenting from Life on the Frontier to the Managed Child*. Princeton: Princeton University Press, 2016.
Franks, Peter. *Print and Politics: A History of Trade Unions in the New Zealand Printing Industry, 1865–1995*. Wellington: Victoria University Press, 2001.
Fussell, Paul. *The Boys' Crusade: The American Infantry in Northwestern Europe, 1944–1945*. New York: Modern Library, 2005.
Fyne, Robert. "World War II: Feature Films." In *The Columbia Companion to American History on Film: How the Movies Have Portrayed the American Past*, edited by Peter C. Rollins, 125–36. New York: Columbia University Press, 2003.
Gilbert, James. *A Cycle of Outrage: America's Reaction to the Juvenile Delinquent in the 1950s*. Oxford: Oxford University Press, 1988.
Ginzburg, Carlos. *The Cheese and the Worms: The Cosmos of a Sixteenth-Century Miller*. Translated by John and Anne Tedeschi. Baltimore: Johns Hopkins University Press, 1992.
Goodnow, Trisha, and James J. Kimble, eds. *The 10 Cent War: Comic Books, Propaganda, and World War II*, Jackson: University Press of Mississippi, 2017.
Gordon, Ian. *Comic Strips and Consumer Culture, 1890–1945*. Washington, DC: Smithsonian Institution, 1998.
Gould, Chester. *The Complete Dick Tracy: Dailies & Sundays*. Vol. 8. San Diego: IDW Press, 2009.
Gross, Gary. *Kid's Stuff: Toys and the Changing World of American Childhood*. Cambridge, MA: Harvard University Press, 1997.
Hajdu, David. *The Ten-Cent Plague: The Great Comic-Book Scare and How It Changed America*. New York: Picador, 2009.
Hanks, Fletcher. *Turn Loose Our Death Rays and Kill Them All! The Complete Works of Fletcher Hanks*, edited by Paul Karasik. Seattle: Fantagraphic Books, 2016.
Hansell, Haywood S., Jr. *The Strategic Air War against Germany and Japan: A Memoir*. Washington, DC: Office of Air Force History, 1986.
Harmon, Christopher C. "'Are We Beasts?' Churchill and the Moral Question of World War II 'Area Bombing,'" *The Newport Papers* #1. Center for Naval Warfare Studies, December 1991.

Harvey, R. C. "A Stretch in the Bone Age: The Life and Cartooning Genius of V. T. Hamlin." *Comics Journal*, May 21, 2012. http://www.tcj.com/a-stretch-in-the-bone-age-the-life-and-cartooning-genius-of-v-t-hamlin/.

Haas, Britt. *Fighting Authoritarianism: American Youth Activism in the 1930s*. New York: Fordham University Press, 2017.

Hultkrans, Andrew. "Steve Ditko's Hands." In *Give Our Regards to the Atomsmashers! Writers on Comics*, edited by Geoff Dyer, 208–25. New York: Pantheon Books, 2004.

Hurt, R. Douglas, *The Great Plains During World War II*. Lincoln: University of Nebraska Press, 2008.

Hynes, Samuel. *The Soldier's Tale: Bearing Witness to a Modern War*. New York: Viking, 1997.

Jacobs, Lewis. "World War II and the American Film." *Cinema Journal* 7 (Winter 1967–68): 1–21.

Jarvis, Christina S. *The Male Body at War: American Masculinity During World War II*. Dekalb: Northern Illinois University Press, 2010.

Jenkins, Henry, ed. *The Children's Culture Reader*. New York: New York University Press, 1998.

Johnston, Patricia. Introduction to *Seeing High and Low: Representing Social Conflict in American Visual Culture*. Berkeley: University of California Press, 2006.

Jones, Gerard. *Men of Tomorrow: Geeks, Gangsters, and the Birth of the Comic Book*. New York: Basic Books, 2005.

Juvenile Delinquency (Comic Books): Hearings Before the Subcommittee to Investigate Juvenile Delinquency of the Committee on the Judiciary, United States Senate. Eighty-Third Congress, Second Session Pursuant to S. 190 Investigation of Juvenile Delinquency in the United States. April 21, 22, and June 4, 1954. Printed for the use of the Committee on the Judiciary; United States Government Printing Office, 1954.

Karasik, Paul. "Die Frogs! The Lost Comics of James Kugler." *Comics Journal* 307 (Winter/Spring 2021): 212–21.

Keegan, John. *The Second World War*. New York: Penguin Books, 1989.

Kimble, James. *Mobilizing the Home Front: War Bonds and Domestic Propaganda*. College Station: Texas A&M University Press, 2006.

Kimble, James. "Spectral Soldiers: Domestic Propaganda, Visual Culture, and Images of Death on the World War II Home Front." *Rhetoric and Public Affairs* 19, no. 4 (Winter 2016): 535–70.

Kirschner, Don S. *City and Country: Rural Responses to Urbanization in the 1920s*. Westport, CT: Greenwood, 1970.

Kohlert, Frederik Byrn. "Working It Through: Trauma and Autobiography in Phoebe Gloeckner's *A Child's Life* and *The Diary of a Teenage Girl*." *South Central Review* 32, no. 3 (Fall 2015): 124–42.

Lederer, Charles. *The Junior Cartoonist—Presenting a Simple Course in Drawing, Painting and Caricature—Combining Amusement and Instruction.* Chicago: Monarch Book Company, 1906.

Lepore, Jill. *The Secret History of Wonder Woman.* New York: Vintage Books, 2015.

Lesy, Michael. *Wisconsin Death Trip.* New York: Anchor Books, 1973, 1991.

Levy, Giovanni. "On Microhistory." In *New Perspectives on Historical Writing,* edited by Peter Burke, 93–113. University Park: Pennsylvania State University Press, 1991.

Lindenmeyer, Kriste. *The Greatest Generation Grows Up: American Childhood in the 1930s.* Chicago: Dee, 2005.

MacDonald, J. Fred. *Don't Touch That Dial: Radio Programming in American Life, 1920–1960.* Chicago: Nelson-Hall, 1982.

Magnússon, Sigurður Gylfi. "The Contours of Social History. Microhistory, Postmodernism and Historical Sources." In *Mod nye historier. Rapporter til Det 24. Nordiske Historikermøde* 3, edited by Carsten Tag Nielsen, Dorthe Gert Simonsen, and Lene Wul, 83–107. Århus. 2001. http://www.akademia.is/sigm/contours.html.

Maier, Charles S. "Targeting the City: Debates and Silences about the Aerial Bombing of World War II." *International Review of the Red Cross* 87, no. 859 (September 2005): 429–44.

Mandaville, Alison. "'Duel. I'll Give You a DUEL': Intimacy and History in Megan Kelso's *Alexander Hamilton Trilogy*." In *Comic Books and American Cultural History,* edited by Matthew Puszt, 59–75. New York: Continuum, 2012.

Marten, James. "Childhood Studies and History: Catching a Culture in High Relief." In *The Children's Table: Childhood Studies and the Humanities,* edited by Anna Mae Duane, 52–67. Athens: University of Georgia Press, 2013.

Matthews, E. C. *How to Draw Funny Pictures: A Complete Guide to Cartooning, with 200 illustrations by Zim,* 2nd ed. 1928; Chicago: Frederick Drake, 1944.

McCalman, Iain, and Paula A. Pickering, eds. *Historical Reenactment: From Realism to the Affective Turn.* Basingstroke and New York: Palgrave Macmillan, 2010.

McCloud, Scott. *Understanding Comics.* New York: Harper Paperbacks, 1994.

McCreery, Stephen, and Brian Creech. "The Journalistic Value of Emerging Technologies: American Press Reaction to Newsreels during World War II." *Journalism History* 40, no. 3 (Fall 2014): 177–86.

Mintz, Steven. "The Changing Face of Children's Culture." In *Reinventing Childhood After World War II,* edited by Paula S. Fass and Michael Grossberg, 38–50. Philadelphia: University of Pennsylvania Press, 2011.

Mintz, Steven. *Huck's Raft: A History of American Childhood.* Cambridge, MA: Belknap Press, 2004.

Moffett, E. Albert. "Hometown Radio in 1942: The Role of Local Stations During the First Year of Total War." *American Journalism* 3, no. 2 (1986): 87–98.

Moon, Michael. *Darger's Resources.* Durham: Duke University Press, 2012.

Morain, Thomas J. *Prairie Grass Roots: An Iowa Small Town in the Early Twentieth Century.* Ames: Iowa State University Press, 1988.

Morlan, Don B. "Slapstick Contributions to WWII Propaganda: The Three Stooges and Abbott and Costello." *Studies in Popular Culture* 17, no. 1 (October 1994): 29–43.

Muir, Edward. "Introduction: Observing Trifles." In *Microhistory and the Lost Peoples of Europe*, edited by Edward Muir and Guido Ruggiero. Baltimore: Johns Hopkins University Press, 1991.

Murray, Christopher. *Champions of the Oppressed? Superhero Comics, Popular Culture, and Propaganda in America during World War II.* Cresskill, NJ: Hampton Press, 2011.

Nickel, Philip J. "Horror and the Idea of Everyday Life: On Skeptical Threats in *Psycho* and *The Birds*." In *The Philosophy of Horror*, edited by Thomas Fahey. Lexington: University of Kentucky Press, 2012.

Overy, Richard. *The Bombing War: Europe, 1939–1945.* New York: Penguin, 2013.

Palladino, Grace. *Teenagers: An American History.* New York: Basic Books, 1997.

Parkinson, Gavin. "Henry Darger, Comics, and the Graphic Novel Contexts and Appropriations." In *The Cambridge History of the Graphic Novel*, edited by Jan Baetens, Hugo Frey, and Stephen E. Tabachnick, 139–54. Cambridge: Cambridge University Press, 2018.

Penry, Jerry. "Nebraska's Fatal Air Crashes of WWII." http://www.nebraskaaircrash.com/main.html.

Pinto, Sarah. "Emotional Histories and Historical Emotions: Looking at the Past in Historical Novels." *Rethinking History* 14, no. 2 (June 2010): 189–207.

Price, Michael H. "V. T. Hamlin and the Road to Moo." In V. T. Hamlin, *Alley Oop: 1939*. Vol. 4 of *The Library of American Comics Essentials.* San Diego: IDW Publishing, 2013.

Pustz, Matthew, ed. *Comic Books and American Cultural History: An Anthology.* New York: Continuum, 2012.

Register, Cheri. *Packinghouse Daughter: A Memoir.* St. Paul: Minnesota Historical Society Press, 2001.

Reynolds, Richard. *Super Heroes: A Modern Mythology.* Jackson: University Press of Mississippi, 1992.

Roeder, George. *The Censored War: American Visual Experience during World War Two.* New Haven: Yale University Press, 1993.

Rollins, Peter C. "World War II: Documentaries." In *The Columbia Companion to American History on Film: How the Movies Have Portrayed the American Past*, edited by Peter C. Rollins, 116–24. New York: Columbia University Press, 2003.

Savage, William W., Jr. *Commies, Cowboys, and Jungle Queens: Comic Books and America, 1945–1954*. Middleton, CT: Wesleyan University Press, 1990.

Schatz, Thomas. "World War II and the Hollywood War Film." In *Refiguring American Film Genres*, edited by Nick Browne, 89–128. Berkeley: University of California Press, 1998.

Schultz, Gladys Denny. "Comics, Radio, Movies: What Are They Doing to Our Children? And What Should Parents Do about Them?" *Better Homes and Gardens* 24 (November 1945): 22–23, 73–75.

Schuyler, Michael W. "The Ku Klux Klan in Nebraska, 1920–1930." *Nebraska History* 66 (1985): 234–56.

Scott, Cord A. *Comics and Conflict: Patriotism and Propaganda from World War II through Operation Iraqi Freedom*. Annapolis, MD: Naval Institute Press, 2014.

Sledge, E. B. *With the Old Breed: At Peleliu and Okinawa*. Oxford: Oxford University Press, 1990.

Slotkin, Richard. *Gunfighter Nation: The Myth of the Frontier in Twentieth-Century America*. New York: Atheneum, 1992.

Slotkin, Richard. "Fiction for the Purposes of History." *Rethinking History* 9, no. 2/3 (June/September 2005): 221–36.

Soper, Kerry "Classical Bodies versus the Criminal Carnival: Eugenics Ideology in 1930s Popular Art." In *Popular Eugenics: National Efficiency and American Mass Culture in the 1930s*, edited by Susan Currell and Christina Cogdell, 269–307. Columbia: Ohio University Press, 2006.

Spaight, J. M. *Bombing Vindicated*. London: G. Bless, 1944.

Spiegelman, Art, and Chip Kidd. *The Complete Maus*. New York: Pantheon Books, 1996.

Spiegelman, Art, and Chip Kidd. *Jack Cole and Plastic Man: Forms Stretched to Their Limits*. San Francisco: Chronicle Books, 2001.

Spiller, James. "This Is War! Network Radio and World War II Propaganda in America." *Journal of Radio Studies* 11, no. 1 (2004): 55–72.

Sterns, Peter N. "Challenges in the History of Childhood." *Journal of the History of Childhood and Youth* 1, no. 1 (Winter 2008): 35–42.

Sutton-Smith, Brian. *The Ambiguity of Play*. Cambridge, MA: Harvard University Press, 2001.

Sutton-Smith, Brian. *Toys as Culture*. New York: Gardner Press, 1986.

Tilley, Carol L. "Seducing the Innocent: Fredric Wertham and the Falsifications That Helped Condemn Comics." *Information & Culture: A Journal of History* 47, no. 4 (2012): 383–413.

Tilley, Carol L. "Children and the Comics: Young Readers Take on the Critics." In *Protest on the Page: Essays on Print and the Culture of Dissent Since 1865*, edited by James L. Baughman, Jennifer Ratner-Rosenhagen, and James P. Danky, 161–79. Madison: University of Wisconsin Press, 2015.

Tilley, Carol L. "Educating with Comics." In *The Secret Origins of Comics Studies*, edited by Mathew J. Smith and Randy Duncan, 3–11. New York and Abingdon: Routledge, 2017.

Tumey, Paul. "The Precisely Rendered Blam: Alley Oop in 1939." *Comics Journal*, September 10, 2014. http://www.tcj.com/the-precisely-rendered-blam-alley-oop-in-1939/.

Tuttle, William M., Jr. *"Daddy's Gone to War": The Second World War in the Lives of America's Children*. New York and Oxford: Oxford University Press, 1993.

Vassallo, Michael J., ed. *Atlas at War!* Russ Heath, Stan Lee, Gene Colan, Syd Shores, John Severin, Don Heck, Steve Ditko, Jack Kirby, and More. New York: Dead Reckoning/Marvel, 2020.

Watt-Evans, Lawrence. "The Other Guys," originally in *The Scream Factory* #19 (1997), reproduced at http://www.watt-evans.com/theotherguys.shtml.

Werner, Emmy E. *Through the Eyes of Innocents: Children Witness World War II*. Boulder, CO: Westview Press, 2000.

Westbrook, Robert B. "Fighting for the American Family: Private Interests and Political Obligation in World War II." In *The Power of Culture: Critical Essays in American History*, edited by Richard Wightman Fox, T. J. Jackson Lears, and Robert B. Westbrook, 195–221. Chicago: University of Chicago Press, 1993.

Whitted, Qiana. *EC Comics: Race, Shock, and Social Protest*. New Brunswick: Rutgers University Press, 2019.

Witek, Joseph. *Comic Books as History: The Narrative Art of Jack Jackson, Art Spiegelman, and Harvey Pekar*. Jackson: University Press of Mississippi, 1989.

Wright, Bradford W. *Comic Book Nation: The Transformation of Youth Culture in America*. Baltimore: Johns Hopkins University Press, 2003.

Wright, Bradford W. "Comic books." *The Encyclopedia of Popular Culture*. Vol. 1, 560–62. Detroit: St. James Press, 2000.

Index

About the Authors

Michael Kugler (PhD, University of Chicago) teaches modern European history at Northwestern College in Orange City, Iowa. He writes primarily on Scottish Enlightenment studies but also publishes on historical narrative and popular culture. His recent work is on providentialist theology and the development of the social sciences in early-modern Britain. His work has appeared in the *Journal of Eighteenth-Century Studies*, *Scotia*, the *Journal of the History of Childhood and Youth*, and *Fides et Historia*. He was recently ordained as a priest in the Episcopal Church of America. This is his first book.

James William "Jimmy" Kugler (1932–1969) was born and raised in Lexington, Nebraska. Part of a large German immigrant community, he attended Lexington schools and was active in football, basketball, classroom art, and wartime activities like scrap metal drives. A year after graduation, he moved to Denver. After meeting Patricia Andrews, they married and moved west, first to Salt Lake City and finally to Portland, Oregon. There they raised three children: Michael, Steven, and Tamara. Jimmy worked various jobs: driving a diaper truck, in the shipping industry along Portland's Willamette River, or in small factories. Patricia separated from Jimmy in 1968, moving with the children to Colorado. A year later, she reconciled with him and planned to return to Portland. Before leaving, Patricia learned that Jimmy, who had broken his leg playing mushball, suffered a series of epileptic seizures from poor medical treatment as well as alcohol abuse. He died in July of 1969.

CPSIA information can be obtained
at www.ICGtesting.com
Printed in the USA
BVHW010249221222
654794BV00001B/2

9 781496 842824